ZODIAC

BERKSHIRE

Edited by Simon Harwin

First published in Great Britain in 2002 by
YOUNG WRITERS
Remus House,
Coltsfoot Drive,
Peterborough, PE2 9JX
Telephone (01733) 890066

All Rights Reserved

Copyright Contributors 2002

HB ISBN 0 75433 526 7
SB ISBN 0 75433 527 5

FOREWORD

Young Writers was established in 1991 with the aim of promoting creative writing in children, to make reading and writing poetry fun.

Once again, this year proved to be a tremendous success with over 41,000 entries received nationwide.

The Zodiac competition has shown us the high standard of work and effort that children are capable of today. The competition has given us a vivid insight into the thoughts and experiences of today's younger generation. It is a reflection of the enthusiasm and creativity that teachers have injected into their pupils, and it shines clearly within this anthology.

The task of selecting poems was a difficult one, but nevertheless, an enjoyable experience. We hope you are as pleased with the final selection in *Zodiac Berkshire* as we are.

Contents

Dedworth Middle School
                Matthew Davies   1

Easthampstead Park School
Louise Hayward	1
Dean Race	2
Lucy Gander	2
Michael Kennedy	3
Joe Harris	4
Amy Rose	5
Beccy Surry	6
Holly Munn-Cocks	6
Thomas Gore	7
Lucy Ray	8
Gareth Barker	8
Joanna Paradine	9
Jemma Spurdle	9
Chris Mitchell	10
Becky Stuckey	11
Becca Duffett	12
Richard Jordan	13
Lewis Reed	14
Jessamy Culley	15
Sam Dunn	16
Cayleigh Tucker	16
Heather Moore	17
Frances Becher	17

Hemdean House School
                Pippa Robinson   18

Holyport Manor School
Peter Edwards	19
Clark Hall	20
Shane Hillier	20
Amandeep Mann	21

Krystal Little	21
Edward Paranathala	22
Ravneet Bassan	22
Shayne Morse	23
Dominic Staker	23
Carlos Pinto	24
Michael Darby	24
Kirstie Hill	25
Stewart McDougall	25
Daniel Clarkson	26
Karen Young	26
Charlotte Lloyd	27
Ben Cripps	27
Alexander Roberts	28
Simon Elliman	28
Barry Grist	29
Craig Dowling	29
Dean Ridley	30
Mary Driscoll	30
Carlos Hazell	31
Charlie Thompson	31
Jacky Marshall	32
Andrew Duff	32
Samir Faruki	33
Lee Hillier	33
Christopher Perry	34
Julie Grant	34
Edward Tucker	35
Colin Barron	35
Rachel Fennelly	36
Jonathan Lewis	36
Dean Tye	37
Greg Rackstraw	37
John Bushnell	38
Matthew Graham	38
Michael Belcher	39

Newlands Girls' School
	Tara Bennett	39
	Ellen Wong	40
	Mary Meanwell	40
	Chloe Edwards	41
	Sadia Rashidi	41
	Stephanie Komen	42
	Rachael Taylor	42
	Tina Chohan	43
	Amreen Ali	44
	Tamsin Levett	44
	Charlotte King	45
	Sinead Urso	46
	Rosemarie Michel	46
	Katy Ellis	47
	Amy Castle	48
	Catherine Spencer	48
	Georgina Allen	49
	Katie Gavin	50
	Charlotte Bryan	50
	Clare Third	51
	Natalie Downing	52
	Lianne Moody	52
	Sophie Temple	53
	Hannah Steel	54
	Amy Nield	55
	Stephanie Haines	56
	Elizabeth E Savill	56
	Anastasia Memmott	57

Presentation College
	Jordan Green	57
	Joshua Walker	58
	Alex Murray	59
	Matthew Rhodes	60
	Luke Krauze	61
	Douglas Shepherd	62
	Bhavin Lad	63

David Reid	64
Elliott Winterbottom	65
Paul Muston	66
Cyril Mitkov	67
Duncan Whittle	68
Michael Rimmer	68
James Shuff	69
James Watson	70
James Bayliss	70
Andrew Lowe	71
Daniel McClure Fisher	71
Andrew Nimako	72
Kenley Morris	72
Jonathan Lewis	73

Reading School

David Liptrot	73
Oliver Mark	74
James Ellis	75
Thomas Fright	76
Christopher Taylor	76
Tom Lax	77
Tom Spindler	78
Henry Hoskins	79
Arangan Nagendran	80

St Gabriel's School, Newbury

Louise Sheridan	81
Caroline Wilson	82
Bronwen Edwards	83
Sophie Davies	83
Chantelle Davison	84
Natalie Hyde	85
Alice Stimey	86
Ailsa McCaughrean	86
Abigail Leech	87
Alice French	88
Angharad Evans	88

Connie Frost	89
Charlotte Bowen	90
Katie Ward	90
Lara Woodhead	91
Emma Constantine	92
Fiona Sim	92
Lucy Karpinski	93
Rosie Bell	93
Alice Staker	94
Pippa Boyd	94
Charlotte Ashwell	95
Vicky Clarke	96
Frances Norris	96
Catherine Ramsbottom	97
Emma Bates	98
Hayley Stalker	98
Emily McMullin	99
Lorna Fisher	100
Charlotte Rogers	100
Nuala Williams	101
Becky Brown	101
Laura Harradine-Greene	102
Beth Tilley	102
Jade Luckett	103
Siân Davey	104
Beth Robertson	105
Abi Goulding	106
Alexandra Vevers	106
Victoria Wood	107
Jennifer Steele	108
Kerry Emery	108
Jaishil Main	109
Natasha Perkins	110
Emily Osborne	110
Rebecca Hilliard	111
Charlotte Gent	111
Zoe Hurst	112
Sarah Rossiter	113

Emma Nickson	114
Lizzy Hartigan	115
Stephanie Poulson	116
Emily Pettman	116
Clare Weaver	117
Laura Fleming	118
Rachel Liddiard	118
Lynette Masters	119
Sophie Kilduff	120
Katie Meek	120
Rebecca Le Flufy	121
Anna Slack	122
Gemma Phillips	123
Sarah Bailey	124
Helen Warwick	125
Hazel Luck	126
Ellie Cleaver	127
Verity King	128
Sarah Duggan	128
Eilidh Totten	129
Nicola London	129
Helen Markides	130
Holly Woodhead	130

Sandhurst School

Kate Fields	131
Clare Beck	131
Natalie Evans	132
Alex Hughes	132
Tyler Honey	133
Rickie Cole	134
Emma Wesley	134
Lucy Sedge	135
Dee Wolfe	136
Matthew Middlebrook	136
Jemma Howard	137
Simon Amphlett	137
Matt Bull	138

Alan Roper	138
Tom Currie	139
Adam Meadway	140
Rachael Arnott	141
Angelo Pascucci	141
Nathan Mulliner	142
Adam Mark Keen	142
Christopher Roderick	142
Josh Scantlebury	143
Daniel Pigney	143
Matt Reynolds	144
Matthew Vickers	144
Kea Hinsley	145
Lauren Hancy	146
Zoe Ford	146
James Histed	147
Annie Ovcharenko	148
Christopher Ibbitt	148
Emma Elliott	149
Tom Osborne	149
Dean Charman	150
Suzanna Sanders	150
Jonathan Fisk	151
Emma Brown	152
Karina Winslade	152
Billy Stevens	153
Sam Oakford	154
Charlene Bailey	155
Jason Amos	156
Sophie Chandler-Smith	156
Lisa Hench	157
Laura Adlington	157
David Charter	158
Natasha Sandy	158
Lucy Davenport	158
Robert Caruana	159
Kaylie Brace	159
Tara Woodhouse	160

Laura Andrews	160
Emma Chandler-Smith	161
Lucy Crabtree	161
Tristie-Alice Handley	162
Alex Elliott	163
Sarah Farrant	164
Stuart Armitage	164
Katie Lowden	165
Keir Boswell	165
Calum Doherty	166
James Phillips	166
Guillaume Evans	167
Kirsty Clarke	168
Alice Bolton	169
Emily Dunford	170
Ben Willoughby	171
Gemma Elliott	172
Katherine Lewis	173
Rose Bradshaw	174
Luke Florey	174
Catherine Kilpin	175
Jonathan Frampton	176
Sarah Charter	176
Philip Jackson	177
Daniel Barreiro	177
Miles Turner	178
Elliott Westrop	178
James Shamtally	179
Shaun Moseling	180
Ryan Gardiner	181
Roger Goff	182
Lauren Dawes	182
Heather McManus	183
Heather McIntosh	184
Hayley Beard	184
George Hayes	185
Emma Diprose	185
Leah Worthington	185

Natasha McGregor	186
Mikayla Field	186
Ben Harrison	187
Jo Gale	188
Amy Fisher	188
Callum MacDonald	189
Luke Hathaway	190
Amber Coneley	190
Hannah O'Neill	191
Kelly Brown	191
Ryan Brown	192
Emily Owles	192
Stephanie Whitcombe	192
Richard Amey	193
Julie Wilson	193
Amy Dunford	194
Simon Mepham	194
Jonathan Moir	195
Chris Foskett	195
Patrice Lilly	196
Sheridon Harmsworth	196
Christian Fahey	197
Alex Koulouris	197
Yvonne Dalton	198
Sarah Wyatt	198
Alannah Smith	199
Mark Turton	200
Jamie-Lee O'Hara	200
Jody Lees	201
James Tidd	201
Sarah-Louise Reed	202
Penny Simpson	202
Carl Lavender	203
Martin Calvert	204
Lauren Floyd	204
Trumaine Odaranile	205
Abigail Tyler	205
Lizzie Goodchild	206

Sarah Hiscutt	206
Stephen King	207
Anna Middleton	208
Robbie Coomber	209
Sam Lord-Castle	210
Andrew Barnes	210
Kayleigh Crew	211
Rachel Bell	212
Jamie Robson	212
Andrew Walker	213
Jade Freeman	214
Michelle Trowbridge	214
Guillaume Klimczak	215
Matthew Alden	215
Caroline Jones	216
Katy Wesley	216
Jessica Gibson	217
Steven McKane	217
Tom Cooper	218
Natasha Gontier	218
Danielle Davis	219
Leanne Sullivan	220
Laura Cooper	221
Katie Avery	221
Kirsty Currier	222
Maxine Girard	222
Leanne Ledger	223
Natalie Smart	224
Marcus Hau	224
Daniel Clegg	225
Liam O'Keeffe	226
Richard Inions	226
Chloe Soane	227
Matthew Hegarty	227
Tom Ashton	228
Charlotte Goodwin	228
Daniel Buckler	229
David Allistone	230

Rebekah McVittie	230
Ellen Whalley	231
Lorna Glazier	232
Rebecca Taylor	232
Fern O'Guynn	233
Roxanne McVittie	233
Hayley Thair	234
Sophie Heffernan	234
James Lowden	235
Hayley Parkinson	236
Matt Bowman	236
Charlotte Rose	237
James Cholerton	238
Laura Brownlie	239
Aimée Sheppard	240
Laurel Knight	240
Rebecca Sandy	241
Antony Walter	242
Stephanie Hayes	242
Laura Rosewell	243
Chris James	244
William Savage	245
Rebecca Driver	246
Hannah Stockley	246
Oliver Lammas	247
Sam Alexander Bennetts	247
Alexander Hurst	248
Sophie Fisk	249
Jack Hicks	250
Elise Crayton	250
Sophie Coster	251
Daniel Nelson	252
Stuart Peter Forbes	252
Daniela Swingler-Brown	253
Katy Gravett	254
Adam James	255

The Poems

THE SECOND WORLD WAR

Dig and dig to build the trenches
All among the awful stenches,
Infantry stand in a foot of water
All awaiting their awful slaughter,
Machine guns rattle
Among the cries of battle,
Dead and wounded line the floor
On what was once a grassy moor,
Forward rumbles a weary tank
On which the insides must have stank,
Under fire more than the rest
Bearing only a British crest,
In the air, bombs are dropped
Will it ever be stopped?
Back on the battlefield, guns are fired
Every soldier is really tired,
Over the front line they will run
Always ready to fire their gun.

Matthew Davies (11)
Dedworth Middle School

BIRD'S LIFE

Starts as fluffy, downy, fuzzball, can't yet leave the nest.
Then the chick learns to fly and becomes an independent bird,
Hopping around your garden and eating all the worms.
Meets a female, courts her and he becomes her mate.
She lays eggs, sits on her nest.
When the eggs hatch, out come fluffy, downy, fuzzballs,
Can't yet leave their nest.
Being fed by their mother and father.

Louise Hayward (13)
Easthampstead Park School

SCHOOL

The bell rings, time for tutor,
Miss has trouble doing the register.

The bell rings for first lesson,
Today we're having a maths session.

Hooray! The lesson ends,
But is the next lesson okay? It all depends.

Time for break, finally I'm free,
I rush to tuck very quickly.

Now third lesson, wicked, I've got French,
We might be sent out to sit on the bench.

Last lesson before lunch, what is it again?
Please not English, I've forgotten my pen.

Now it's lunch, I'm going home,
I've gotta come back, but I'd rather go to Rome.

Last lesson of the day, I've got PE,
It's pretty cool, except for rugby.

School ends and it's raining,
But luckily I've got football training.

Dean Race (13)
Easthampstead Park School

MONDAY MORNING

Monday morning,
I'm in a dream,
My old alarm clock starts to scream.

I look a mess,
My hair's a state,
If I don't hurry I will be late.

I can't find my tie,
I can't find my book,
I don't have any time to look.

My teacher will say,
'You're late again.'
Don't you agree,
School is a pain.

Lucy Gander (13)
Easthampstead Park School

THE FLIGHT OF ICARUS

My gentle wings are my limitless escape,
from the inferior limitations of man's basic anatomy.
The afternoon breeze, an elegant dancer of hope,
does a majestic waltz, timeless and beautiful through
fleshy, naked arms of mine.
My curious mind is unable to describe, the everlasting,
soaring flight of immortals.
I can fly and I can glide, rising up into swirling clouds,
God's comforting pillows are my expansive soul.
My flight of fantasy is like the sky around me,
infinite, vibrant and lustfully breathtaking.
I tease and caress the burning fireball above,
as it is a precious audience, to my euphoric performance,
of flight, both mystical and nervously revealing.
A dream of a simple child is now a man's delight.
Fantasy now reality.
I am more elegant than the cooing dove,
stronger than the steel-like eagle, and
more beautiful than the vibrant macaw.

This moment is forever.

Michael Kennedy (14)
Easthampstead Park School

THE JOURNEY ACROSS THE PLAYGROUND

As I step onto the black plain,
I cast my gaze across the playground,
I see a Year 7 boy in pain,
A gang of his friends gathered around.

I stride forward carefully,
To avoid a flying football,
And notice a gang of tough kids,
Celebrating their victory by the wall.

I see an argument break out,
About a basketball player who's a cheat,
I behold a girl running about,
And one having something to eat.

Then I view the playground ogre,
Whom I must defeat,
To reach the picnic area,
And the friends that I must meet.

The punch from his huge club-like fist,
I parry with mine,
His second jab missed,
At that point I was doing fine.

He gave me an evil grin and then,
Knuckle-dusters and all,
His scruffy 'mates' charged into the fray,
And my confidence began to fall.

I decided flight was better than fight,
So before being beaten several different blacks,
I called, 'Look, there's a footballer, Sam Knight.'
And ran when they had turned their backs.

I scampered across the playground,
And dived behind a tree,
A respite I had found,
Friends and sanctuary ahead of me.

Just 100 metres to safety,
But the thug's breath I could almost smell,
They were closing in behind me,
Then thank God! There goes the bell!

Joe Harris (13)
Easthampstead Park School

MY TYPICAL SCHOOL DAY

The bell rings and I'm ten minutes late
My hair is a mess and my uniform's a state
I burn myself in cooking, I fall over twice in dance
I've done my essay wrong for English, can I have another chance?

In maths I get all my equations wrong
In music I'm left with a bell, ding-dong
In science my hand hurts from writing too much
I do hurdles in PE, is that not enough?

My geography teacher is terribly dressed
So everybody laughs and she gets stressed
History's no better and as the minutes go by
They feel like boring hours, I wish that I could cry.

Once again it's been a tiring day
They need to be much shorter I'd say
I can finally go out and chat with my friends
My typical school day has come to an end.

Amy Rose (13)
Easthampstead Park School

DARKNESS, LIKE A . . .

Darkness,
Like an endless pit.
Sunshine,
Like the dazzling rays.
Sadness,
Like a broken heart.
Happiness,
Like a cheerful smile.
Running,
Like a tiring race.
Walking,
Like a constant march.
Crying,
Like a pitiful sob.
Laughing,
Like a hearty chuckle.
Whisper,
Like a hushed murmur.
Shouting,
Like a thundering roar.

Beccy Surry (12)
Easthampstead Park School

PARENTS

Parents are so annoying,
They always have loads of rules,
Don't do this and don't do that,
And you can't wear that to school.

Look at all of that make-up,
Go and wipe some of it off,
Don't use your hands you silly girl,
Go and get a warm, damp cloth.

You can't go out with that boy,
He's way too old for you,
If you disobey me young lady,
I'll ground you for a week or two.

Parents are so annoying,
Don't they have anything better to do
Except for moaning at kids all day,
To say their please and thank yous?

Holly Munn-Cocks (13)
Easthampstead Park School

SPAIN

If you go to Spain
You'll feel the heat
Scorching the hairs
On the back of your neck
You'll see the cacti
Barbed with nails
The huge green lizards
They'll scare you to death
At the beach you'll see
The barbies are burning
The crashing of the waves
As they hit the soft sand
If you look out far
In the distance you'll see
Boats of all kinds
In that big blue sea
So appreciate Spain
And the wonders it holds.

Thomas Gore (14)
Easthampstead Park School

SHOPPING

Money, money, money,
I can't wait to spend,
I'm walking down the street,
Just me and a friend.

Clothes, clothes, clothes,
I love to try them on,
I must spend wisely,
My money's nearly gone.

Money, money, money,
I'm all spent out,
I won't ask for more,
'Cause my mum will scream and shout.

Clothes, clothes, clothes,
I wish I could buy more,
But my mum will kill me,
I know that for sure.

Lucy Ray (14)
Easthampstead Park School

SNOW FALLING

Snow falling is icing sugar,
Scattered on the world,
Snow is a giant ghost,
Asleep on the world,
Snow that falls is cotton balls,
For kids to play around all day.

Gareth Barker (12)
Easthampstead Park School

FIRE

Fire is a bright light,
Shining in the night,
Fire is the morning sun,
Shining over the hills.

Fire is my form of heat,
On a cold winter's night,
Fire is a light bulb,
Lighting up my life.

Fire is the warm colour,
Shining from the rainbow,
Fire is the redness,
In a demon's eyes.

Joanna Paradine (12)
Easthampstead Park School

CLOTHES

Clothes, clothes, clothes,
It's all I think about.
I spend, spend, spend,
Until I start to shout.

I look, look, look,
At all the clothes that I see.
Until I find something
That fits me perfectly.

I'm poor, poor, poor,
At the end of the day.
I'm not looking forward
To the bills I have to pay.

Jemma Spurdle (14)
Easthampstead Park School

SONGS

Craig David wants to
Rendezvous,
Human Nature thinks
He Don't Love You No.

Wyclef Jean calls
911,
And Lolly thinks,
Girls Just Want To Have Fun.

Boom! Are
Falling
And J-Lo's
Love Don't Cost A Thing.

Bob The Builder want
To fix it,
Wu Tang Clan sings
Gravel Pit.

Safri Duo are
Played A-live,
The Warp Brothers
Will Survive.

Dums Dums are an
Army of two,
Dido wants to say
Thank You.

Robbie Williams wants to
Let Love Be Your Energy,
Oxide And Neutrino think you're
No Good For Me.

Martine McCutcheon's
On The Radio,
DJ Luck and McNeat are doing the
Piano Loco.

Chris Mitchell (13)
Easthampstead Park School

AT THE CINEMA

Can't wait till tonight,
Going out with my mate,
How long will
She make me wait?

We're going to the cinema,
Going to watch a movie,
We'll get a box of popcorn,
And a strawberry smoothie.

We walked into the room,
Adverts on the screen,
Me and my friend
Are so very keen.

Bang, crash, wallop,
The door slams shut,
The lady in front
Gave an awkward tut.

It's time to go,
Never mind,
We'll get some snacks now,
Let's see what we can find!

Becky Stuckey (14)
Easthampstead Park School

A Speech By The Totally Impossible Party

If you let me run the country,
The country will be fun,
Fun will be the country,
The country will be fun!

People will drive safely,
Safely through the rain,
The rain will stop completely,
I'll completely stop the rain!

People will be happy,
Happy they will be,
They will be so happy,
Happy faces you will see!

So when you place that tick,
Tick that box of mine,
My ideas are best,
So tick that box of mine!

If you let me run the country,
The country will be fun,
Fun will be the country,
The country will be fun!

Becca Duffett (14)
Easthampstead Park School

WIMBLEDON

Wimbledon, Wimbledon,
Those speeding shots!
They definitely have speed,
It never stops!

After they serve,
The rally starts,
The players are ready,
And the ball's like a dart!

Tim Henman smashes it!
You must be careful!
I'm so nervous!
Because the scores are level!

The match is almost over,
Because it's match point!
Tim Henman serves,
And scores another point!

Tim Henman wins!
He just got an ace!
He's done well,
Because he's got first place!

Richard Jordan (13)
Easthampstead Park School

FRIDAY

Science, oh what a bore,
I can't be bothered to listen no more.
I look at the textbook in vain,
Damn! Not forces again.

Maths I've got now,
It's such a row.
Teachers shouting,
Children fighting.

English, with Miss Davies,
Please God, please save me!
She says I'm a poet,
And I don't even know it.

Now my favourite lesson, art,
I have a painting I have to start.
Blue, red, yellow and brown,
I love the feeling of paint flowing round.

The joyful lunchtime!
Now I've eaten, I feel fine.
I go on the library computer,
A few minutes later it's time for tutor.

The last lesson is PE,
A good sportsman I must be.
I'll do my best at tennis,
I'm so good, it's total bliss!

I'll go home now, no more school!
Home alone. Yes, it's so cool!

Lewis Reed (14)
Easthampstead Park School

UNTITLED

A averted a nasty accident
B behaved in an unbelievably odd way
C couldn't find her next class
D denied having anything to do with the science explosion
E enjoyed running in the playground
F focused on finding the tuck shop at break
G got told off
H headed to the playground
I imagined life at his old school
J jumped at the chance to experiment with Bunsen burners
K kicked his football over the wall
L limped to the office
M managed to escape from school
N's naughtiness landed him in a fight
O overcame many obstacles
P's politeness helped him very much
Q queried the point of school
R recorded a piece of music
S surveyed hundreds of shouting children
T taunted children smaller than herself
U 's ultimate memory was locking a teacher in a cupboard
V ery lazy, didn't complete work
W's wacky sense of humour gave her lots of friends
X xperienced a wild day
Y yelled at the top of his voice
Z zigzagged along the path.

Jessamy Culley
Easthampstead Park School

AT THE SEASIDE

The whippy wind whined in pain,
The selfish sea screamed aloud,
The fast fish flustered furiously,
As the golden sun shone brightly.

The seagulls shrieked sharply in the calm sky,
The hungry harbour dragged ships onto the shore,
The seashells shone on the glistening sand.

The jet-skis zipped across the white-tip waves,
The bold rocks stared out to sea,
The shaky grannies soaked up the sun,
As the sun went down.

Sam Dunn (13)
Easthampstead Park School

SCARED

Alone at night,
Hearing the howls of wolves,
The moon glaring,
As the mist covers the sky,
Footsteps pass,
Scary shadows cover the trees,
Seeking red eyes,
Scratching noises screech,
Scared stiff, almost paralysed.
Scared!

Cayleigh Tucker (13)
Easthampstead Park School

Snow

Each flake of snow is a little falling star,
Falling and falling, inch deep on every car.

The snow covers the world like a big white blanket,
Soft, warm and thick like a giant marshmallow.

The icicles are daggers hanging everywhere,
Glistening and shining so much that people stop and stare.

The snowballs are water bombs splattering everywhere,
And the snowmen in their hat and scarf are standing there almost bare.

The clouds are curtains that the sun is opening,
The snow begins to melt and soon trickles away to nothing.

Heather Moore (12)
Easthampstead Park School

Fire

Fire is the sun,
Burning bright.
The flames are grass,
Growing in the light.
The wood is food,
Feeding the fire.
Smoke is its breath,
Drifting up higher.
The ashes are the body,
The fire is dead.
The ashes are the blood,
That the fire has bled.

Frances Becher (13)
Easthampstead Park School

WHAT A CHANGE

Time and again I look round this room,
And think of the time I could spend,
Spiralling on a downward flume,
That just doesn't seem to end.

Slowly as life at school gets worse,
The hurt they cause they cannot see.
I wish that I could end this curse,
That has been put upon me.

Teachers cannot stop the pain,
To help, friends don't even try.
What do these torturers have to gain?
Nothing but to see me cry.

So here I am with these new friends,
Reliving my torture and pain,
And finally I feel like my person blends,
And life just feels all right again.

Now things are different, I'm happier, see,
My family has noticed my smile.
Everyone said it was them not me,
But to see it, it took me a while.

Pippa Robinson (15)
Hemdean House School

FERRARI MOTORBIKES

I like Ferrari motorbikes
Because they are cool
Zooming down the motorway
Breaking every rule

You don't need to queue up
In the traffic jam
They shoot down the middle
As fast as they can

They are red and black
Shinier than any car
I don't know why
But they're the best by far

Maybe it's the engine
Or maybe the exhaust
But I like my Ferrari motorbike
Better than a Porsche

I can give a Jaguar
A run for its money
I'll be so far ahead
It'll be very funny

Riding my Ferrari motorbike would be a breeze!

Peter Edwards (12)
Holyport Manor School

ELVIS

Elvis was a singer
He sang all different songs
He grew up in Memphis
And he became a movie star

He starred in lots of movies
My favourite's 'Kissing Cousins'
Elvis plays two parts in this
With blond hair and with black

In 'GI Blues' he plays a soldier
And he fights in a war
He's stationed in Germany
And he beats up his friend

I listen to his songs all the time
I can pretend to be him.

Clark Hall (13)
Holyport Manor School

CARS

They're fast
They're cool, they are used for banger racing
They crash, and smash up
They don't use doors in banger racing
They race
Around the track
Number 33 wins!

Shane Hillier (11)
Holyport Manor School

DAD

Dad is funny and kind
He's grumpy some of the time

Dad is clever and bright
He gives lots of hugs at night

Dad has lovely dark brown hair
Sometimes he's a bossy bear

Dad is very special to me
He's as happy as can be

Dad is tall, dark and slim
And I really love him.

Amandeep Mann (14)
Holyport Manor School

MYSELF

My name is Krystal
I am good at spelling
I am good at geography
I learn
I like PE
Sometimes I get stressed
I bang my head
I get angry
I never hit anybody
Just myself.

Krystal Little (15)
Holyport Manor School

PAT

Pat tells us to brush our teeth
She tells you off if you do something wrong
She sends you to bed early
She shouts and nags lots and lots.

But . . .

She smiles when we are good
And takes us out to lots of places
I like going to the leisure pool best
She helps us with our homework
She reads to us
She does lots of great things.

Edward Paranathala (14)
Holyport Manor School

MY FRIEND HAYLEY

Hayley is my best friend
She is helpful
She is funny
She is nice
She has ginger hair
And light brown eyes
She is beautiful
Hayley is my best friend.

Ravneet Bassan (11)
Holyport Manor School

KELLIE IS MY WITCH

Kellie is a witch,
She puts a spell on me,
To make her toast and jam,
And a pot of tea.
She howls, screams and bites,
She gives everyone a fright.
On her broomstick she does fly,
Up into the moonlit sky.
Spiky hair, a crooked nose,
Where she hides, nobody knows.
Bright long red razor-sharp nails,
For her dinner she eats gooey snails.

Shayne Morse (13)
Holyport Manor School

BANGER RACING

Smashing the cars
Damaging them
Crushing and crashing them
Banging different cars
The colours are bright red
Blue and green
Skidding the muddy dirt track
Like you have never seen
Clashing and banging
The cars speed round
Smashing and crashing
Into the ground.

Dominic Staker (13)
Holyport Manor School

SILENT HUNTER

He waits like a leaf, waiting to fall off his tree
He waits for his prey
To come to him
Patient he must be
He moves quickly and quietly.
He attacks from the trees
He puts his paws on his prey, digging his five inch claws
Into his now feeble prey
This animal has no fear
He has no weakness
His camouflage is perfect for his hunting ground
The name strikes fear into the heart of the animal kingdom
This amazing animal is the leopard.

Carlos Pinto (15)
Holyport Manor School

MOTORBIKES

Motorbikes are cool
But scrambling is fun
Every weekend
Come rain or sun
Going over mud tracks
Going over jumps
Getting all muddy
Hitting all the bumps
Losing concentration
Is dangerous to do
You'll fall in the mud
And get covered in goo.

Michael Darby (13)
Holyport Manor School

ME AND MY MUM

My mum does a lot
She does the cooking,
Ironing, washing, cleaning.
I make her a coffee.
She is a happy person.
We go out to a club.
We play bingo.
She won!
She made a happy noise!

My mummy is a good woman.
She is a friend.
She is my best mummy!

I look after my mummy.
Sometimes I do the table.
I put on knives and forks.
I put on place mats.
I put on sauces.
We enjoy our meal together.
She is my best mummy!

Kirstie Hill (15)
Holyport Manor School

ROCK

I like rock, you can see I'm a grunger,
I thrash my keyboard till it's fit to drop,
Papa Roach, Limp Biskit too,
These monster sounds vibrate the ground.
Out on the town in my Bolts.
Rock rules, okay!

Stewart McDougall (11)
Holyport Manor School

MY DAD

My dad
Had an accident
He was
On his bike
At the light
Waiting
For it to go green
It was red
A man went through
And hit
My dad
The ambulance came
The siren was loud
He hurt his back
My dad is best.

Daniel Clarkson (15)
Holyport Manor School

GIRL GUIDE

My name is Karen
I enjoy all the Girl Guide games
At the end of meeting we sing the tap song
At the start of meeting, we go in patrol
There are four patrols
I am in the Kingfisher patrol
I go to the disco
Sometimes I go to Prior Close
I miss the Guides on Friday night
When my mum picks me up.

Karen Young (14)
Holyport Manor School

STUART AND MYSELF

Stuart was my friend
He was a caretaker
We laughed together
When they told me
The news
I was in shock
Next day in English
We were talking about 'myself'
I was sat there
Tears were in my eyes
I had to go out
In the Christmas play
He gave me a cuddly toy
He made me forget
I am disabled
He was my friend.

Charlotte Lloyd (15)
Holyport Manor School

MY MUM IS COOL

Mums are cool
They give you food
They make your bed
They wash your smelly socks
They keep you good
They take you shopping
They take you swimming
They take you bowling
They take you ice skating.

Ben Cripps (12)
Holyport Manor School

THUNDERBIRDS

They live on Tracey Island
Waiting for emergency calls
Thunderbird 5 stays in space
And monitors the Earth.

Thunderbird 1 is always fast
And always arrives on time
At the danger zone
Waiting for Thunderbird 2.

Thunderbird 2 carries the equipment
Thunderbird 3 goes into space
Last but not least, there's Thunderbird 4 and 6
4 goes into water and 6 rescues people.

Thunderbirds fight the baddies
And rescue the world
The Hood always loses
But he always comes back.

Alexander Roberts (11)
Holyport Manor School

THE RACING CARS

I wish I could have a racing car
And race round the track
And beat Schumacher
And win the race
My car would be blue
But Schumacher would catch me up
And a car would crash into Schumacher
And I would win the race.

Simon Elliman (11)
Holyport Manor School

MYSELF

Miss Victoria Lee
Moving to Colnbrook
She's going to put a lick of paint
On her house
She'll then come over to see me.

I live in Colnbrook
I live with my nan and grandad
As well as my younger brothers.

I have a mum, dad, half brother and grandad
I am the eldest
It's difficult being the eldest
I'm expected to look after them.

When I am eighteen I will leave home
I'll follow my nan
I'll work in the hotels
I've already had one work experience
I know what it's like
I have found a lot of people
I like there.

Barry Grist (15)
Holyport Manor School

TRAINS

I like riding in trains,
Looking out of the windows
At other trains passing us,
And seeing lots of houses.
The train stops at the station,
Stewart's there to meet me.

Craig Dowling (11)
Holyport Manor School

MYSELF

I don't like school much
I did like it
When I did
My work experience
I worked at Legoland
I did landscaping
I cut the grass
I moved Lego and sand
I was there 10 minutes
I got breakfast
Not like here
Paul asked me to do stuff
I did it
I liked doing it
Not like here
I want to go out to work.

Dean Ridley (15)
Holyport Manor School

SWIMMING

The water is cool
In the outdoor pool

The water is fun
Especially in the sun

Splish, splosh, splashing everyone
This is great fun.

Mary Driscoll (13)
Holyport Manor School

MYSELF AND KARATE

I watch 3 Ninja videos
I buy karate clothes
I learn karate
Boxing
Fighting
It's good for the body
It's exercise for me to be fit
Not for hurting people
I started in the summer
Boxing and breaking wood
I watch a film about karate
I learn about big jumps and climbs

I like it, but I don't use it
Against people.

Carlos Hazell (14)
Holyport Manor School

OLIVER

My cat is called Oliver, sometimes I call him Olly.
He likes to sit in the sink and play with the water.
My daddy shouts at the cat and he runs away.
I think although my daddy shouts, he loves Olly anyway.
He has tuna to eat and milk to drink.
I can pick him up and stroke him.
Olly really loves me and I love him too.
I wish I could take him to school with me.

Charlie Thompson (15)
Holyport Manor School

MYSELF AND FOOTBALL

Saturday was a special day
I went to Manchester
I actually saw Man United play
It was great
They scored 4 goals
Ole Gunnar Solksjaer
I remember!
I looked at half-time
The scoreboard said
'Today's attendance is
50,000,565!'
When I saw it, I just
Could not believe it!
The noise!
The crowd was so loud.

Jacky Marshall (14)
Holyport Manor School

LOTTERY

Buy a ticket
They pick the machines and the balls.
Mix the balls up
Wait for the numbers to be drawn
Press the button
Mix the balls up
Six lucky numbers
And one bonus ball.

The winner.

Andrew Duff (13)
Holyport Manor School

LET THE MONKEYS HIT THE FLOOR

Monkeys are cheeky, they steal stuff
Let the monkeys hit the floor
Let the monkeys hit the floor
They like bananas and fruits
Let the monkeys hit the floor
Let the monkeys hit the floor
I like monkeys but one day
They will get too cheeky
Then they will hit the floor
Let the monkeys hit the floor
Let the monkeys hit the floor
Let the monkeys
Hit the floor.

Samir Faruki (14)
Holyport Manor School

I LIKE PLAYING FOOTBALL

I like playing football
With my friends
We go to the Astro Turf
In Bracknell
There are about ten of us
They are people I like being with
Richard is kind to me
We buy each other stuff
Like drinks and stuff
We were making a tree house
I got stuck
He had to help me down.

Lee Hillier (15)
Holyport Manor School

CHEEKY AND CHEERFUL

C heeky and cheerful
H elping with Children In Need
R elaxing in my garden I like to do
I am interested in reading comics
S weets are nice to eat when I am in a bad mood
T rouble sometimes
O n the pitch
P erry's family are the best
H appiness and sadness makes you cry
E veryone said happy birthday to me
R elaxing and listening to music

P eople have laughs and jokes
E veryone loves me when I am polite
R ock and roll music when I am in a good mood
R eally scary movies are excellent
Y ippee when it is the end of term!

Christopher Perry (15)
Holyport Manor School

MR BEAN

'Mr Bean The Movie' is my favourite film
He is really funny.
Mr Bean is good at school and he sees all his friends.
He has black hair
Brown eyes
And an ugly face.
He always wears a tie
And some sensible shoes.

Julie Grant (12)
Holyport Manor School

MYSELF

I'm Edward Tucker
My subjects include English, Maths, PSE and so on
I live near the railway and I call myself a train spotter
Please do not call me Harry Potter
In my spare time I play on the computer
It's not fitted with a hooter
I don't always allow my trains to be documented
Sometimes facts and figures are depicted
Although it is my passion
TOPS numbers and things are restricted
I listen to music sometimes
Mainly from Beatles and Oasis
Some songs are explicitly bad
With swearing at an awful basis
Effectively I play computer golf
Hoping the golf ball gets there
Then I play different card games
Including Hearts, FreeCell and Solitaire
In fact, I'm entirely useful at anything!

Edward Tucker (15)
Holyport Manor School

RENAULT

They're fast and they're comfortable
They're colourful
They're big and spacious
And they are
Bouncy
And they are
Leathery
And their faces are cute on a car.

Colin Barron (12)
Holyport Manor School

ME AND MY MUM

I live with my mum and David
My mum has black hair
She goes shopping with me
On Saturday and Sunday
Sometimes we go to the park
It's sunny
I like having a story
Because Mum reads to me
She makes her voice change
It's funny
Sometimes it's sad too.

Rachel Fennelly (15)
Holyport Manor School

DADDY'S MOWER

Daddy's mower cuts the grass
It makes a noise
Daddy's mower sounds very loud
It scares me
Daddy's mower is red
He pulls the handle
The grass smells when it's been cut
I like the smell
The grass is green
I like the colour.

Jonathan Lewis (13)
Holyport Manor School

HALLOWE'EN

A ghost is spooky
A ghost is scary
A ghost is white
A skeleton is bony
A skeleton is white
It jumps out at night
And gives you a fright
A monster is hairy
A monster is green
Witches do spell on
Hallowe'en
The living dead come out on
Hallowe'en night.

Dean Tye (12)
Holyport Manor School

FORMULA 1

Warm up lap,
Wait at the starting line,
Racing drivers with their helmets on,
Waiting for the starting lights,
Fast cars and sponsors,
All wanting the trophies,
So fast we hit the safety barrier,
The safety car comes out,
Pit stop for repairs,
The chequered flag at last,
The champagne and the money's mine!

Greg Rackstraw (13)
Holyport Manor School

MYSELF AND WWF

I like WWF
I like the Rock and Kurt Angle
It was amazing at the Unforgiven
The crowd were everywhere,
They cheered!
The Rock is pretty tall
He says a lot of good stuff.
Like 'I'll kick your candy . . . !'
Kurt has an ankle lock.
They give up.
I would give up!

John Bushnell (15)
Holyport Manor School

MATHS

Maths, what a muddle!
Take away that and add this.
My goodness!
Division is an even bigger muddle.
Divide that core.
Blow that.
Multiplying is worse.
It gets on your nerves.
End of lesson.
What a blessing.
Time for play.
Hooray.

Matthew Graham (14)
Holyport Manor School

BOATS

Boats are big,
Some boats are small,
They can be long and narrow,
Or wide and tall.
Speedboats are the best,
Sea-spray in my face.
We're faster than the rest,
We will win the race.

Michael Belcher (11)
Holyport Manor School

WISPA

She's black and white, furry and bright
She's been trained to do agility all night.

She likes to run, walk and skip
She likes to chase balls into a ditch.
If she does not find that ball
She'll cry all night, going bawl, bawl, bawl.
And if she doesn't find that ball
You'll never know where it's gone at all.

Have you guessed yet . . . are you right?
If you think it's a human you're well out of sight
But if you think it's an animal you're very bright.

Is she a horse? A cat? Or a frog?
No, she's Wispa, our next door neighbour's dog.

Tara Bennett (12)
Newlands Girls' School

THE MIRROR - PETRACHIAN POEM

A pure glass that reflects.
It's not what it seems to many.
Look inside and see what's there, a Helix.
A hidden form that's hard to find, a lost soul.
A thief of reflections, never knowing its true form.
Always lonely with no heart or life of its own.
Inside the illusion appears. Not seeing the real thing.
A shadow is there. Imitating the body. Like an act of same actions.
The shining object is as clear as crystal and water.
The image returns when faced in sapphire drops of rain.
Full of mystery, no one knows if it has true and deep feelings.
The answer is never there. Only a question and puzzle remains.
Another dimension. Very unknown, like fog swirling.
No clue where it's going. Mystery unsolved.
It's the light, the worst enemy of night.

Ellen Wong
Newlands Girls' School

I LOVE SWEETS

Sweets are my favourite things.
When I see them my heart sings.
Mars bars, Bounty, Cadbury's bar.
Black Jacks stick to my teeth like tar.
Soft toffee, hard lolly,
Are always in my shopping trolley.
Sweets, yum, yum, they fill my tum.
Sweets are my favourite things.
When I see them my heart sings.

Mary Meanwell (11)
Newlands Girls' School

BREAKFAST, LUNCH, DINNER, OH NO!

When you eat your dinner tonight,
Think of me eating my mushy peas,
I have to eat it or I have it for breakfast,
Oh please.
My mother makes me eat it and says,
'It's good for your eyesight.'
And I say okay, just to be polite.

When you eat your breakfast tomorrow
Think of me eating my brussel sprout,
I have to eat it or I have it for tea,
I look at it and my lips just pout.
My mother says, 'It's good for your knee bone,'
I look at her and give a slight groan.

When you eat your lunch today,
Think of me eating my - ham, egg and chips
My mother says, 'As you've been such a good girl,
You can have a treat,
But it's mushy peas for dinner,
Now come on, take a seat.'

Chloe Edwards (13)
Newlands Girls' School

LOVE

Love is gold and red
It smells like a gift from Heaven
It tastes like golden crispy chicken
It sounds like a violin played in the heart of a peaceful man
It feels like a warm and fresh blanket
It lives in every heart of every living thing.

Sadia Rashidi (11)
Newlands Girls' School

THE WRITER OF THIS POEM!

The writer of this poem
Is smaller than a tree.
As fast as a cheetah,
As greedy as can be.

As strong as a wrestler,
As sleek as a cat.
As lazy as a hippopotamus,
And that's the end of that.

As quick as lightning,
As loud as a loud noise.
As light as a bulb,
As naughty as the boys.

The writer of this poem,
Is as fast as a flash.
And is quite hard to find,
Because she's off in a dash.

Stephanie Komen (11)
Newlands Girls' School

THE WRITER OF THIS POEM

The writer of this poem
Is cleverer than a computer
As wise as an owl
As patient as a recruiter

As fast as a cheetah
As strong as an ox
As keen as the rain
As cunning as a fox

As clear as water
As bright as the sun
As tricky as a knot
As loving as Mum

The writer of this poem
Is perfect all through
She's one of a kind
But this might not be true!

Rachael Taylor (11)
Newlands Girls' School

THE WRITER OF THIS POEM

The writer of this poem
Is smaller than a door
As funny as a comedienne
As clean as a floor

As fresh as a flower
As bright as a star
As hungry as a hippo
As fast as a car

As kind as a mother
As soft as a feather
As cheeky as a monkey
As strong as some leather

The writer of this poem
Would never chop a tree
She's one in a million
And she always will be!

Tina Chohan (11)
Newlands Girls' School

WAKING UP

She jumps up, swerves around the desk,
She reaches the drawer,
Puts on her school uniform.
She reverses to the door
And zooms straight for the bathroom.
But wait, her brother's out too,
Will she make it? No, I don't think it's likely . . .
But she leaps,
She dodges,
And she's made it into the bathroom first!
She brushes her teeth, does her hair and she's out.
She slides down the stairs,
Just misses her dad,
And runs straight for the kitchen.
She grabs the milk, Cornflakes and
She goes for the bowl,
Dodges the chair,
Slam dunks her lunch into her bag,
Whizzes for the front seat in the car.
Warning . . . brother's coming too.
She leaps, he leaps,
She dodges and she lands a perfect landing.
She's first and holds the world record
Of seven minutes and thirty seconds!

Amreen Ali (11)
Newlands Girls' School

HALLOWE'EN

Devilishly we walk with our bags
Faintly recognising who is who
Sedately we ring their door bell
Gradually they open the door.

Viciously we shout at them
Grimly, 'Trick or treat,' we cry out
'Give us something nice to eat,'
Cruelly we take the sweets from their hands
Hurriedly we run to the next house.

Tamsin Levett (13)
Newlands Girls' School

THE CLOUDS, SUN, MOON AND SKY

Fluffy, white pillows
In the velvety blue sky
In all different kinds of shapes
They make me wonder why.

A yellow beach ball
Of fluffy fire
As we circle it
It becomes our heart's desire.

The bright blue carpet
With a small yellow ball
I sometimes ponder
Why it does not fall.

The giant splodge
Of bluey-white paint
Who put it there?
It makes me feel rather faint.

The sun is smiling down below
The moon sleeping while the pillow fights
As they race across the sky
The sun cries out in delight.

Charlotte King (13)
Newlands Girls' School

THE WRITER OF THIS POEM

The writer of this poem
Is as pretty as a princess
As elegant as an elephant
It's hard to confess

> She's as wild as a whale
> As playful as a puppy
> She loves being on stage
> Her little teddy is called Cubby

She gazes at the stars
And stares at the moon
She sleeps on her magic carpet
And flies on her broom

> The writer of this poem
> Is still very young
> She's enjoyed this adventure
> (But it's only just begun).

Sinead Urso (11)
Newlands Girls' School

THE WRITER OF THIS POEM

The writer of this poem
has got the biggest house
she's got one million maids
but she's as quiet as a mouse

The writer of this poem
gets everything she desires
but sometimes . . .
she's as stressed as flat tyres

The writer of this poem
is as busy as a bee
writing up stories
to enjoy in our dreams

The writer of this poem
although busy is as calm as a lake
I wonder what her dream was
when she awakes?

Rosemarie Michel (12)
Newlands Girls' School

THE WRITER OF THIS POEM

The writer of this poem
is as proud as a peacock
as intelligent as a dolphin
and as friendly as a horse

She is soft and gentle
she is as sharp as a knife
as tall as a tree
and has her own life

She is kind to nature
she is as strong as metal
and never cried
even when she was stung by a stinging nettle

The writer of this poem
would make people stunned
she is one out of a million, maybe a billion
(even when she hummed).

Katy Ellis (11)
Newlands Girls' School

AT THE END OF THE YEAR

At the end of the year,
Hats, gloves and coats come out,
It's getting cold, without a doubt!

At the end of the year,
Lakes freeze over with silver tops,
And the temperature surely drops!

At the end of the year,
Reindeer prancing,
People dancing!

At the end of the year,
The sky drops snow,
And along comes a bearded man who we all know!

At the end of the year,
Snow is crunching,
Children munching,
Their Christmas pie,
As they look up into the sky
And watch robin redbreast fly by!

Amy Castle (12)
Newlands Girls' School

THE WRITER OF THIS POEM!

The writer of this poem
Is smaller than a flea
As cool as a cucumber
As pretty as can be.

As funny as a jester
As free as a bird
As quick as lightning
As noisy as a herd.

As funky as a monkey
As bright as a star
As cute as a baby
As speedy as a car.

The writer of this poem
Is as sneaky as can be
The writer of this poem
Is not me!

Catherine Spencer (11)
Newlands Girls' School

THE WRITER OF THIS POEM

The writer of this poem
Is as busy as a bee
As messy as a rubbish tip
As wild as the sea

As cool as a freezer
As smooth as ice
As fussy as a peacock
As quick as a slice

The writer of this poem
Is quick on her feet
Is as noisy as an elephant
As sticky as a sweet

Has dark hair as smooth as silk
Which flows and flies
Is as happy as a hippo
And has hazel, happy eyes.

Georgina Allen (11)
Newlands Girls' School

Hallowe'en

Hallowe'en is spooky,
The magic words are
Looky mooky pooky.

    The night is full of mysteries,
    Be careful where you go,
    Oh no, where are the door keys?

Dress up for the night,
But the monsters could be out,
They might give you a fright.

    Lots of sweets to eat,
    Keep them to yourself,
    It's your own little treat.

The children say . . .
'Trick or treat?
Smell my feet,
Give me something good to eat!'

Katie Gavin (11)
Newlands Girls' School

The Ghost

    Craftily the lonely ghost crosses the field,
    Swiftly over the old farm wall,
    Gently past the farmer's sheep,
    Eagerly past the sleeping dog.

    Cunningly through the farmhouse,
    Up the stairs and through a wall,
    Boldly into the farmer's room
    Suddenly with a *boo!*

Charlotte Bryan (12)
Newlands Girls' School

FIRE

Spitting, soaring, searing, great,
A flickering, fiery, fierce snake.
Crackling, churning, crying galore,
Burning bright, battling for more.

A devil dancing and singing a song,
Cackling and laughing merrily along.
A range of colours, orange and yellow,
That deceiving, dreadful, evil fellow.

Powerful, vivid, bewitching, divine,
A criminal committing crime upon crime.
Scarlet, crimson, amber, red,
Energetic, lively, certainly not dead.

Adventurous, angry, brave and bold,
Blistering, scolding, anything but cold.
Hostile, hungry, huge and hurling,
Like a monster, terrorising, blood-curdling.

Ghostly, fatal, an enraged God,
Infuriated by a poke and prod.
Dynamic, duelling, doomful, loud,
Brilliant, sparkling, stands out in a crowd.

Vivacious, intelligent, crafty and clever,
Fast and forceful, to lose is never.
A carnivorous, mighty dinosaur,
With bloodstained teeth and bloodstained claw.

A murderer in every right,
Killing with vigour, killing with might.
Ranting, raging, rapid and raving,
Not burning out until filling its craving.

Fire.

Clare Third (13)
Newlands Girls' School

My Treacherous Love

The night was young and the trees were swaying,
When I saw my love in the moonlight, standing cold and still,
The light through the trees was painting the road with ice,
But my love was still there, alone and silent,
Her hair swaying softly in the breeze,
Her eyes were stark and distant in a sea of love and anger,
She was wearing black, black and red,
Her lips moved gently, she sung softly to herself,
She thrust her hand deep into her pocket,
Deeper and deeper until her hand pulled it out,
Her hand pulled out my death warrant,
It shone black in the moonlight,
Then she pulled her finger back on the trigger,
I did not think to stop her,
I fell silently onto the road,
She stood shaking, not daring to breathe for fear of discovery,
She ran to my side, kneeling carefully on the ground,
Her hand rested on my heart,
She picked up her hand and looked at it shining red,
She let out a silent cry and fled into the darkness.

Natalie Downing (12)
Newlands Girls' School

A Poem About How I Feel At My New School!

I'm not scared anymore,
I want to go to school once more,
I love it at my new school,
I think it's really super-cool!

In the uniform you get very hot,
It is seriously bad, (not!)
I've made lots and lots of new friends,
If anything happens it always mends!

Lessons really aren't that bad,
But all my friends call me mad!
I felt worried about going when I was in year 6,
But when you're there you think it must be a fix!

Well, it really wasn't good timing,
With all the things in New York,
It's very interesting, I mean all the talk,
But it is very exciting starting a new school, try it!

Lianne Moody (11)
Newlands Girls' School

EATING DINNER

Mum's just about to start dinner here at Conker Avenue.
It is exciting as Jamie Brown pulls himself back
To avoid the temptation.
Five minutes through, can he hold it in?
No he can't!
He rushes downstairs, there's a clatter as he does.
But no, it's not ready, wait, hang on, he's ,
He's asking if he can lick the spoon, he must be desperate.
And the answer is no, what a disappointment.
Jamie is staring into space, oh dear, he has to clear the table.
He is clearing extra quick to make Mum go faster,
The dinner's being served and he reaches for the gravy,
Splats it on, *delicious.*
He's picking up a carrot and in it goes.
He's finished in world record time.
Well done Jamie and that's all from us here at 4 Conker Avenue.
Bye!

Sophie Temple (11)
Newlands Girls' School

Sun

The sun.
A bright star in the daylight zone
The closest to Earth,
    Yet still alone.
Like a glowing candle that never goes out
The magic glory,
    The Druids shout.
Its shape is an infinite size
It looks down on us,
    Its shininess wise.

The light.
How mystically you shine down on me
Most experimented,
    Most left be.
I wish to be as bright as you
Most great,
    Through and through.
I look to the sky and wonder
Where is your smile?
    I ponder.

The magic.
Your powerful grand witchcraft
Is trapped like a child
    In a mine shaft.
Stronger than the mirror moon
When it's up,
    Sun will come soon.
The sun is the great medium star
Some venture to go,
    I won't go that far.

Hannah Steel (12)
Newlands Girls' School

IN THE WARTIME PATHS OF DOVER

Like a muddy footprint
On a beach of golden sand,
Or like a bloodstained cut
On a child's tiny hand.

The figure in the night gown
The gown light blue all over,
Standing in a closed doorway
In the wartime paths of Dover.

A translucent soul that's standing
With a candle all alight
Ready to go to sleep,
Although it's barely night.

And then a gnarled finger
Is beckoning at me,
The guide leads the party into a room,
There'll be an explanation maybe.

He tells us nothing, really
Just some meaningless facts,
We're just getting led out of the room,
When wait, there's a catch!

He warns us that there is
A form of immortality
People think it's their imaginations,
But really it's reality.

I still believe I saw a ghost,
Although some people think I'm insane,
I was just so scared of the wartime ghost,
I'll never go back into the tunnels again.

Amy Nield (11)
Newlands Girls' School

THE WRITER OF THIS POEM

The writer of this poem
is as quick as a flash
as small as a snail

She's as clean as a glove
as pretty as a butterfly
as fresh as a fruit

She's as smart as a calculator
as tall as a giraffe
as busy as a bee

She's one in a million
she's one of a kind
the writer of this poem cannot be me!

Stephanie Haines (11)
Newlands Girls' School

AUTUMN LEAVES

Falling like rain
Swish, crackle and sweep
Smelling like fruit
Bare, cold trees
Looking like people
A carpet of leaves
Like fur on the ground.

Elizabeth E Savill (11)
Newlands Girls' School

NESSIE

As I walked along the shore, my dress billowing out behind me,
I looked upon the ever-changing surface of the loch,
And wondered what laid beneath it.

I saw slight ripples upon the loch as it arose from beneath,
It had scales all over, the mysterious beast.

The colour of the beast was like oil upon water,
I looked up its long neck to its face bathed in sunlight.

Its eyes were a mysterious blue and it made me think
They held many, many secrets.

It vanished from sight, never to be seen again,
Now when I look upon the loch I feel that every move I make
Is being watched by Nessie, the mysterious beast.

Anastasia Memmott (11)
Newlands Girls' School

TRAGEDY

It felt like I had just been stabbed in the heart
by a cold, sharp dagger.
I was as scared as an ostrich
with its head wedged into the ground.
The plane hitting the Twin Towers was like a bird
smashing painfully into a French window.
The plane seemed to scream as it hit the building,
causing destruction, devastation and doom.

Jordan Green (13)
Presentation College

THE PHOENIX

As it stood there,
Tall and proud
Its red-gold feathers glistening,
Glistening
Amongst the windblown
Autumn leaves
And as I stood there
Watching it,
My dear,
It inclined its fiery head
To me
And from its maw
It did issue forth a song,
A song more powerful or
Beautiful than
The sun on the sea;
Or the swirling mists
Around a willow tree.
And then did it open its
Wings
Those wings of awesome
Colour
So blinding were they
To me
That I was forced to avert
My eyes you see.
But this I did only for
A second as my gaze
Adjusted
I saw it there in the sky,
Shining as the very light
Above the horizon, just
After dawn,
A brilliant, blazing
Fireball

All yellows, oranges
And reds
And then 'twas gone
In the blink of an eye
As though it had never
Been.

The bird of fire and song.

Joshua Walker
Presentation College

THE JUMP

'I dare you to do an exell and land it,'
'Bet you I can!'
'Go on then, do it,'
'Fine I will.'

When I took my turn my stomach was a cage with butterflies in
Blood was pounding in my ears like a drum beat
The bike felt like a chariot going into battle

I swung the bike round with the speed of light
As I started to build up sped it felt like an elephant
As I took the corner I felt the back wheel slide as if on ice

As I hit the ramp I felt like a ghost
Like a bird in the sky
Then with a small shock I realised what I had to do
I twisted the handlebars first left then right
And just as I straightened them I hit the earth with a thud
And the soothing sound of the air releasing from the suspension
To me it felt like the kiss of life
The jump was over too soon, I wished I could fly on forever.

Alex Murray (12)
Presentation College

ALONE...

Here they come again,
These tormentors of my mind,
Stalkers of my dreams,
They sit and watch, uncaring,
Unmoved by the plight of this man,
This man alone.

This man,
This man,
This man.

This man. It is now derogatory.
While once we clamoured to be called it . . .
Now these, these things, they break it down,
They remove it, destroy it.
For our generations are sheer memories, data.
Save for this one man.
This man alone.

Still they sit, unmoving, uncaring.
Even they must see the pain, the anger, the hate, the sorrow,
They do.
They see it with a scientist's eye, recording, categorising, noting.
Emotion doesn't exist.
They don't see past the skin, they don't stare in.
To this man alone.

This man who lost it all.
Family, friends, enemies.
Once we were the masters.
Once I was the master.
And now what am I?
I am alone.

Were we better?
Can I say?
I do not know.
I will never know.
For I am truly, and utterly
Alone.

Matthew Rhodes (14)
Presentation College

A PLANT

The seed sits in the earth like a peanut ready to be eaten
The surface of the earth crumbled as if it had been beaten

A root shoots out
And so does the sprout

So the race to the surface has a beginning
Plants trying to get a piece of the winning

Stones around look like an old man's eye
And this gives the plants something to despise

The shoot grows tall
To get the winner's ball

It's trying to get to the finish line
To get a piece of the winning wine

It gets to the top with a shout and a cheer
But instead of wine or beer it finds something queer
Water.

Luke Krauze (13)
Presentation College

NANNY'S SHOES

These are the shoes
My nanny used to wear,
On warm, summer days,
On cold, winter days,
Always happy in these shoes,
Making other people happy
In these shoes.

Going on walks to feed the ducks,
Always getting her shoes muddy,
Then cleaning them until you
Thought they were new,
Praying in church
With these shoes.

Crying tears on these shoes,
Smiling with her shoes,
Eating in smart restaurants
With her lovely smart shoes,
Queuing for a Big Mac
In these dear, familiar shoes.

Sitting on a park bench
Watching me while I play,
Pushing me in my pushchair
While my sister ran away.

Leaving them tidy in the hall
While she cleaned my shoes
Until they too were neat.

The shoes blossomed in the spring,
Shone in the summer,
Froze in the winter,
Turned muddy brown in the autumn.

Warm by the fire, cold in the ice,
Loud in the crowd, quiet as mice,
They tiptoe through the park,
They kick the leaves.

The shoes became redundant,
For they were no use in hospital,
But now my nanny has
Gone to heaven,
And still the shoes live on.

Douglas Shepherd (12)
Presentation College

THE DRAGON

The dragon's wings blow wind around the world
The dragon huffs and puffs as smoke comes out of his nose
The dragon fires a round ball as if it was the blazing sun
The dragon defeats soldiers one by one as they come
The dragon whips his tail to the soldiers as if they were slaves
The dragon runs like a dog into its cave when it starts to pour with rain
The dragon eats the leaves as he tries to stand the pain
The dragon tries to sleep as his nightmare overcomes him
Then one day a villager came with a sword and some armour
The dragon looked in hunger as he whipped his tongue
                                             across his mouth
The man had no fear as he raised his sword
The dragon rose high to mount his descent to fall from the skies
                                             like torpedoes from planes
The man jumped to the side and swung his sword with all his might
What was left was the head of the dragon
The man took the head of the dragon and held it up to the light
To show his people that he had done right.

Bhavin Lad (12)
Presentation College

SURVIVOR

I survived the wolves,
Only to be placed in his Hell hole,
The source of jokes, the eyesore in the landscape,
The laughing stock of my superiors.

Along came the next bunch,
Another mental torment.
I can feel my sanity
Being sucked away by evil beings.

The storyline has been set,
Where's a superhero when you need one,
You in need, dying a slow, painful death,
All alone, you against the world.

'The last surviving human',
Not such a good thing when you call,
Some bars your home, and some aliens, master,
Some pulp food, and some Martians visitors.

I should be allowed to roam free,
And do as I know how.
Follow the influences of my ancestors,
And reclaim the land for my own.

My life means nothing,
Just a 'dumb old human'.
Nothing important,
Just the last in a long line of importance!

David Reid (14)
Presentation College

THE SLY FOX

The fox is smart
The fox is keen
But never ever will the fox be seen

He stalks his prey
With no delay
Waiting for the moment to strike

All farmers despise
Those quivering eyes
After the foxes return

But this time it's fate
As the farmer will wait
For the fox to step in the pen

With a bang he is dead
The fox lost his head
Inches from his dinner delight

The fox's blood was as red as a rose
It squirted out like a fireman's hose
Making a river of death on the lawn

With night as black as a cat
The farmer waits with his baseball bat
For another criminal to call.

Elliott Winterbottom (13)
Presentation College

SPECIMEN

Why do they do this?
Just look at me,
As if I'm something special.
I'm not though - anything special.
I'm not anything like them, though
I wish I was
Like them.
I wouldn't be in this cage,
I would be free,
Free.
With no animals to chase me,
No staring,
Especially no bars.
Just me and freedom.
No one else, just me.
Sadness washes over me
Like a stone being consumed by a river.
I feel like a bird,
Trapped in this cage,
Which is more like a chicken shed.
Small,
Confined,
Tiny.
I feel claustrophobic,
I feel bad,
I feel lifeless,
I feel as if I want to
Die.

Paul Muston (14)
Presentation College

KEEPERS

Why war?
Why?
No war.
'No war,'
   I said.
Why did we do it?
You were
        poisoned
The past haunts again.
But now there's only me to haunt.
Progress,
        is it?
Hunts us,
Puts us in cages,
And calls itself
Progress?
We were poisoned
              or is it progressed?
They too
   will be poisoned.
It's kindness.
More like progress.
I'm tired of being a specimen,
To be looked at,
Talked about.
Be kind,
Enough,
Dismiss me,
       progress me,
             kill me.

Cyril Mitkov (14)
Presentation College

MY POEM

Once there was a man who had women troubles.
His head was out at sea
He walked along not knowing what was going on
And he fell into a puddle.
His face was as wet as a fish.
He tried to think about other things -
So he looked at the sun as he got to the beach.
He saw a huge, yellow beach ball
And he realised how much like the sun it was.
The trees whispered as the three year olds played
With feathers, ferns and Fido the dog.
He looked away and saw a nice girl.
His heart started beating quicker.
He clicked his fingers, and a throbbing in his head hurt
As the beach ball rolled on the ground next to him.
The lady looked up and saw him.
There on the floor was a symbol - he cared.

Duncan Whittle (13)
Presentation College

SNOWY DAY

It's a wonderful day today because it's snowing,
I hope it will keep on going.
I'm running through the woods like a cunning swift fox,
Or jumping up and down like a gazelle.

Suddenly I run into a tree,
The bark as crinkled as an old man's skin.
With the height of a giraffe,
I climbed up like a slithering snake,
Then started swinging from branch to branch,
Like a monkey with speed and agility.

I jumped down and started running again,
Running, running, like a cheetah.
Until I came to a halt and saw a boulder in a river,
Like an elephant bathing in a lake.

Michael Rimmer (12)
Presentation College

POETRY OF WARFARE

Heads down, struggling to walk or see,
Choking on the clouds of smoke,
Wading through the trenches,
Escaping the front line and no-man's land,
Worn to the bone, desperate to sleep,
But not forever . . .

Then came the dreaded noise, the gas was here,
The blurred noise of an officer warning us,
Too slow, one man in agony,
Burning inside, choking on his own blood,
He is coming towards me, pleading and screaming,
His eyes roll, as he is the first to rest . . .

Carrying him away, but then giving up,
The pleas rang out as the bombs rained down,
The once dry trenches now collapsed and soggy,
Staring out into the night sky, brightly lit
By the constant firing of shells,
The musty, dead smell of death all around fills the air,
Bodies half stuck in the quagmire of mud
Limp and riddled with bullets.
I want to run but there is nowhere to go,
I turn to realise I am now on my own,
So I step out over the top, fulfilling my destiny . . .

James Shuff (14)
Presentation College

NEW YORK
(Built 1966-1977. Demolished by terrorist attack on September 11, 2001)

In New York, everyone knows,
The tragedy that happened a few weeks ago.
Two ordinary passenger planes,
Headed to the towers;
They were blown up along with the showers.
As President Bush prepares for war,
The towers crash to the floor.
The death toll no one knows,
They think a definite million or so.
As more and more people are dying,
Fewer planes are flying.
Everyone knows the 11th of September
The day of tragedy everyone will remember.

James Watson (13)
Presentation College

WEATHER POEM

On a cold day
The children went out to play.

The wind is whispering to them
As they climb the tree's trunk.

There is snow falling from the sky
Just like rain does.

The power in the children's legs
As powerful as a lion's jaw.

James Bayliss (13)
Presentation College

The Skateboarder

The boy was like a gymnast,
Skating on the ramp,
The boy was as small as an ant
Compared with the ramp
Which was as big as an elephant,
The boy on the skateboard
Was like a yo-yo,
Going up then down.

On the way home,
He finds some steps, dead ahead.
He attempts to jump them on his board,
He leaps and lands,
Like a cat jumping out of a tree.

Andrew Lowe (12)
Presentation College

My Car

As the wheels span,
I began to wish that the car was mine.
The beaming lights,
The sparkling glass,
The car I saw was frightening and fast.
It stuck to the road like superglue,
But it moved like it was on ice.
In a way it was like a cheetah,
'Cause it was sharp, cunning and clever.
I never thought I would see this
But now I have, it's been bliss.
My dreams to see it have come true,
But I wish I could own it so my hopes would come true too.

Daniel McClure Fisher (13)
Presentation College

ME

I act like my dad
But laugh like my mum
Play football like my brothers
And get a big head like my sister.

Apparently I chatter like a magpie
And have skinny arms like a giraffe
I am as light as a feather
And that's why I run like a jaguar
I sleep like leaves whistling
I've got small feet like an insect
And I sing like a bird.

I love hanging out and playing.

And that is typically my life and me.

Andrew Nimako (12)
Presentation College

THE GAME

The ball has been at the other end all game.
As hard as a ball.
The football is like a rugby ball,
Out of shape.
You can hear the ball bouncing
Down the other end.
The goalkeeper stayed in his goal
Not a shot to save.
A hit or a bounce or a goal.
The goal brings peace.

Kenley Morris (13)
Presentation College

A Railway Station

Down at the station
a flash of light
coming from the distance
roars past me at the speed of a hare
noisier than a jack hammer.

Followed by a distant horn
coming along as quiet as a mouse
as shiny as mercury
it speeds past me.

Jonathan Lewis (13)
Presentation College

Memories

Memories like echoes
Of a time left behind
The innocence of childhood
The fun of the teen years
The seriousness of middle age
Or memories of a beautiful painting
Or of a distant land
Memories of your five senses
The sight of beautiful landscapes
The hearing of musical perfection
The smell of exotic spice
The taste of tropical food
The feel of mystic pattern
Memories can be good but can also be bad
It depends on how you lived your life
And what you want to remember.

David Liptrot (12)
Reading School

BEAUTY AND UGLINESS

Oh no! It's the Citroen 2CV,
One of the ugliest cars in the industry.
To many it is known as the up-turned pram,
They say inside, four you can cram.
Its hideous body shape, bolted together,
Four basic seats, but never in leather.
Banks of aircraft style instruments, not a chance,
Don't forget, they were made in France.
You know you are moving when the scenery changes,
Usually slowly but who knows, there's no gauges.
Unsightly lights stuck out on stalks,
Drive past and everyone talks.
It rolls around corners on its bicycle tyres,
Enjoying the ride - they've got to be liars.
Roll top canvas roof allows in the sun,
Or carrying large objects never out-done.
Five million were sold of this classic car,
But of the Porsche will it go that far?

What a cracker, a stunner, a ravishing machine,
The Porsche Boxster, boy, it's mean.
Its three litre engine, runs like a dream
As it moves it purrs when others would scream.
Alluring colour and elegant shape,
There's nothing to beat the beauty of this make.
Computers on board and seats in leather,
Aerodynamically you'll get nothing better.
Lights shining ferociously in the night,
Even in the dark it's a beautiful sight.
The curvaceous body of a prize machine,
This is the one in which to be seen.

Oliver Mark (12)
Reading School

PRECIOUS FEW

Precious few caught the first ride,
Aren't you glad we survived?
I'm still in denial.
Only survivor, the driver, passed out for a while.

The rain hasn't touched us for days
In this beautiful place,
That we can't afford . . .
Everything's turning out nice and it's making my heart soar.

Precious two saw the first light,
Aren't you glad that their sight
Was open to view?
So all of their traits and mistakes could be passed on to you.

The rain hasn't stopped now for days,
Ever since we became
So tragically flawed . . .
I watched as they took you away and it's making my heart sore.

Precious through all of my life
You can stay if you like,
Exploring my mind.
I tell you it's over and over again I have lied.

As chaos explodes in a shell,
You have kept it so well:
Unblemished and pure . . .
I know what I saw with my eyes, I won't say what my heart saw.

James Ellis (16)
Reading School

THE MYSTERIOUS HOUSE

This house had an eerie feeling of peacefulness,
A spooky creak in the doors,
A boy delivers papers there,
As quickly as a cheetah,
As silent as a mouse.

The silhouettes of the bats killing their prey,
The dying cry for help,
One man, insane, people say,
With a ghoulish grin of the ghost.

The dreaded look of the sinister front yard,
And the realistic look of the stone statues,
It gives me the creeps
Every day of the week
As I pass the mysterious house!

Thomas Fright (11)
Reading School

RAIN

How much rain is in the sky?
There can't be too much more!
At first I didn't mind it much
Then it came through the door.

It seemed to start so long ago
It's pattering caused a din.
I didn't realise at the time
It wanted to come in!

I've had about enough of this
How dare you barge on through!
Go back from whence you came
The sea will welcome you.

Christopher Taylor (12)
Reading School

ANOTHER DAY

Alas another year has gone
be sure there are many more,
but never give up, always carry on.
In whatever you do,
remember happiness is the best.
With each day,
love yourself more, not less.
Live each new twenty-four hours
as if it were your last.
Take everything slow
don't do things too fast.
Pity yourself a little
but not too much.
Make others smile,
never lose touch.
Days will pass by,
being calm is the key.
But for now and forever,
you will have love from me.

Tom Lax (16)
Reading School

RAPING THE GARDEN

The locusts come.

Antennae: flick, flick; wings: crackle, crackle,
An all engulfing, ever consuming, always killing
Orange crackle.

Pulsating swarm flops
Down. Inescapable decent.
Liberators of Moses call in the debt.

Scabbing the landscape
But no healing - only
Scars.
Spreading, gorging, screaming, flowing,
A mould creeping out over lush green skin.

Razing the garden,
Scouring Tunde's cassava pot dry,
Matricidal offspring of nature,
Gnawing the proffering hand.

Familiar?

Tom Spindler (16)
Reading School

THE UGLINESS OF WAR

Cold, grey, bleak, black,
Are the crude machines of war.
Their ugly shapes misfigure the land
As they pull toward the edge.

The edge of the cliff of life
Looms near,
Below is black as pitch.
If over the edge the Earth
Is pulled,
Every life shall end.

As will the lives of those who
Toiled to make those black
Machines.

They forged them with their
Powerful mind,
The driving force of evil.
Now those minds are at the wheel
And nothing can destroy them,
Till they themselves destroy the
Earth.

Henry Hoskins (13)
Reading School

COMPANIONSHIP

My friends and I are all captains,
We all have our own boats,
And cast upon the sea of life
Is where all of our boats do float.

The current may be strong
And the winds keep blowing on
Trying to pull us apart.
My friends and me,
Have no respect for the sea.
We only follow our hearts.

The stronger of us through storms do protect,
Others of us in tasks do perfect,
Together we are a mighty force,
Though through it all love is our source.

The fishing is good,
The fishing is bad,
But we never blame one another.
We share in our wealth,
We stave off bad health,
And give thanks to God and each other.

And if our ships should drift,
Or find themselves some way off course,
We'll cast our ropes and pull them in,
Because unity will be our force.

Arangan Nagendran (13)
Reading School

THE SEASONS

The summer sun dances through
The happy sunflower.
Blades of green grass flicker
In the gentle breeze.
White fluffy clouds bounce across
The pearl-blue sky.
This is *summer*.

The ground is on fire with
Red, yellow, orange, brown leaves.
The blood-red sky, one evening,
Tells a story of its own.
The fighting wind's battle against
The thin bare trees.
This is *autumn*.

The ground turns a fairy tale white,
The sun shimmers across the ice.
The freezing wind
Wraps his cold fingers around
Our ghostly white faces.
Snowmen stand proud in their place.
This is *winter*.

Fluffy white lambs leap for joy
In the fresh new day.
Snowdrops and bluebells put a smile
On anyone's face.
A small plant pokes its head amongst
The land.
Gentle raindrops fall.
This is *spring*.

Louise Sheridan (12)
St Gabriel's School, Newbury

THE MUSTANG

Galloping freely through vast open spaces,
Just the wind through our manes and the thunder of our hooves,
We are happy here.
We are wild, we are free,
We live only by the whispers of the wind,
The echoes of the mountains,
The voices only we can hear.

Screams of panic, ropes flying,
There's human intruder riding a horse
He throws a rope around my neck.
The world's a blur of nothingness.
He pulls me over. He's got me.

Tiny space, human shouts, cracking of whips,
Spurs digging my sides, metal in my mouth,
Leather tied tightly around me.
I'm a prisoner, they're trying to enslave me.
I won't let them.
I'm out of here!

He won't give up, he's after me.
There's a gorge ahead. I have no choice.,
I will not go back to that terrible place.
This is it; I've reached the end.
I leap.
I'm falling, falling, falling . . .
But no . . . I now have wings!
I will fly to a place where no one can catch me.
I am free, forever free.
I live only by the whispers of the wind
The echoes of the mountains,
The voices only I can hear.

Caroline Wilson (11)
St Gabriel's School, Newbury

SNOW

He covers the ground with his white blanket,
The cold bitterness tingles up your spine.
And when he's here everyone knows:
Winter's coming.

He reminds everyone of greyness and poverty,
He gives you chilblains, coughs and colds.
And when he's here everyone knows:
Winter's coming.

Children play with him, they throw him about,
Rosy cheeks contrasting with his whiteness.
And when he's here everyone knows:
Winter's coming.

Bronwen Edwards (11)
St Gabriel's School, Newbury

THE MOON IN HIS KINGDOM

There he is, reflected in your eyes
All misty in the second world above,
The moon and his subjects around him
The cold bane of the night upon
his shoulders
In constant war with the clouds
A clear reign is what he needs to
light the sky
He sits in his throne room of
soft, black velvet
His children twinkle brighter than all.

Sophie Davies (11)
St Gabriel's School, Newbury

THE TRIO

They appeared on the dawn
of a brand new morn,
when the sun was just arising.

Down in the meadow,
I saw the trio,
riding on their midnight steeds.

Their deathly white faces,
their deep red capes
sent quivers down my spine.

But I knew why they were coming!
Oh yes!
I knew why they were coming.

They were coming to get
what belonged to them once,
but now belonged to me!

As they now quickly cantered
down the track,
racing towards my home.

I felt an urge to protect
what now rightfully belonged to me,
instead of belonging to them.

So I flung open the door
and started to run
far away from the trio.

I only ran because I knew
that if they caught me they'd take it.

What used to belong to them,
but now belonged to me,
the precious gift that was
'Life'!

Chantelle Davison (11)
St Gabriel's School, Newbury

JACK FROST

Jack Frost was in the garden
I saw him there at dawn
Jumping, leaping, running,
Prancing on the lawn.

Crystal-white and pearly,
damp, cold and crisp.
Grasping, clutching, sweeping,
covers everything in mist.

He had a cloak of silver,
and a hat of shimmering white.
A wand of glittering crystal
and shoes of winter's light.

Jack Frost was in the garden
But now I'd like to know
Where has my buddy gone to
I've hunted high and low.

Next morning he'll be back here
in his hat of shimmering white.
So it must remain a secret
where he goes at night.

Natalie Hyde (11)
St Gabriel's School, Newbury

SUPERSTAR

Would you be a superstar?
Watched night and day,
The click of the camera,
The only way?

Would you be a superstar?
The pressure's on you,
Be it singer, actor, or TV star,
Could you do it too?

Would you be a superstar?
Stuck upon the stage,
Trying to shout the words out,
That are written on your page?

Would you be a superstar?
Think about it hard,
Without your friends and family,
It could be very hard.

Alice Stimey (11)
St Gabriel's School, Newbury

ALONE

The darkness encircles me,
The crescent moon hangs high,
'The wolves are hunting, my child,'
Owls hoot as night draws by.

The golden eyes of animals
The darkness of the sky,
'The evil ones are near you, child,'
Snakes hiss as night draws by.

The trees sing amongst themselves,
Their rumours and their lies,
'They're after you, my little one,'
Mice squeal as night draws by.

The crowing of the cockerel,
The clock sings its simple song,
'The time has come, my little one,'
The wolves say as I run.

Ailsa McCaughrean (11)
St Gabriel's School, Newbury

THE PONY

She sniffs the air,
She paws the ground,
She rolls on her back,
And look what she's found.

A little frog jumps,
Onto her nose,
Tickles her whiskers,
Gets scared and goes.

She hauls herself up,
With a great big sigh,
Then gallops around,
Her head held high.

She stops at the gate,
Her owner's in sight,
It's time for food,
And stable for the night.

Abigail Leech (12)
St Gabriel's School, Newbury

THE OLD MAN OF THE WOODS

The old man of the woods -
I ruled once - supreme
My gnarled trunk,
Now bent over with age,
Is furnished with lichen
Encrusted, resembling the barnacles on an aged whale.

Ivy's tenuous tendrils wrap around my bulk,
Torturing and throttling the sap out of my veins.
No longer does the woodpecker come knocking on my door.
No more does the crisp carpet of bracken bow down in reverence.
I am brittle like toffee and twisted like barley sugar.
Vibrant colours now dim, misted and mellow.

I think of my youth days where there was an explosion of vitality.
But the Grim Reaper has visited, telling me my time has come.
Many a storm I have witnessed and endured,
A safe place of refuge I have been
But this night the sky, electric and white,
One stab of the fork and I smoulder in two.

Alice French (11)
St Gabriel's School, Newbury

SOUNDS

The ping of the microwave
The chiming of the clock
The beeping of the timer
On the cooker clock.

The swishing of the washing machine
The trickle of the tap
The squirting of the washing up liquid
The purring of the cat.

The sizzling of the sausages
The hum of an oven fan
The sound of murmuring voices
The click of a hissing can.

The thudding of cupboard doors
The chopping of the carrot
The clang of knives and forks
The squawking of the parrot.

What a normal morning!

Angharad Evans (11)
St Gabriel's School, Newbury

AUTUMN

Autumn,
The rain pelting down upon the ceramic roofing,
The bronze coloured leaves fluttering past the double glazed windows.
Cracks in the pavement fill with raindrops,
So much water you feel you may drown.
Splintered branches begin to split as the apples fall to the ground,
Pointed blades of grass are lush green no longer.
Ball-shaped conkers in their threatening shells disappear from
their trees,
Gently they roll down the hill to serve their purpose as food for
passing squirrels.
Winter is drawing closer at last,
Summer drifts away into the sunny past.

Connie Frost (14)
St Gabriel's School, Newbury

My Worst Nightmare

The shutters crashed against the window
As the wind came tumbling through,
The lightning struck and hit a tree
Is it going to fall? This can't be true!
Rumble went the thunder
As if it were hungry for me.
Crash to the ground
Fell an old oak tree.
A branch fell through the window
And set the curtains alight.
The curtains dropped to the floor and
Changed to orange from white,
The fire lashed and thrashed on the floor;
It was creeping quickly out through the door . . .
I gathered myself up with all my might
Tripping down the stairs full of fear and fright.
The fire was like my shadow
Following me everywhere
I knew the fire would catch up with me
As it followed me down the stairs,
Could I reach the door in time
Or would I be too late?
I turned and gasped, red and yellow,
Would this be my fate?

Charlotte Bowen (11)
St Gabriel's School, Newbury

Season

When autumn comes at summer's end
And leaves once green become a blend
Of reds and browns, that fall to Earth,
We think ahead for spring's rebirth.

Dark evenings, grey skies,
Warm houses, apple pies,
Numb fingers, blurred eyes,
Shivering children laugh and cry.

Katie Ward (14)
St Gabriel's School, Newbury

THE ATTIC

They're talking about the attic,
Not me, my mum and dad,
Why are they talking about the attic?
I hope it's not something bad.
I'll know what they're saying one day,
I say,
I'll know what they're saying one day.

There's something in the attic.
Totally hidden from me,
I wonder what's in the attic
That only my parents can see?
I'll know what's in the attic one day
I say,
I'll know what's in the attic one day.

The thing that's in the attic
It's making a funny sound,
Whatever is in the attic
Is bouncing all around
I'll go into the attic one day
I say,
I'll go into the attic one day.

Just not now.

Lara Woodhead (11)
St Gabriel's School, Newbury

GERMS

Readers, be careful, watch and beware,
They come all the time, it's not very fair.
They rest on your hands and on your knees,
They rest on your favourite, delicious toffees.
And when you eat your mushy peas,
You must watch for the fleas.
Bacteria multiplies on the fish,
It multiplies more when it's in the dish.
You can see them when they are found,
But be careful because they're around.
Every day and every night,
They are still trying to fight.
But they get put in a pie,
And very soon they will die.

Emma Constantine (12)
St Gabriel's School, Newbury

DREAM HORSE

In the field of my dreams
he runs around
madly, sweetly, he covers the ground.
His skin is smooth, sleek
and shining
The star on his brow reflects
the moon.
I wish I could ride
this beautiful friend
But in the end, it's only a dream.

Fiona Sim (11)
St Gabriel's School, Newbury

AUTUMN DAYS

Waking up on an autumn day
The red beams of fire burning through my window
As I peer out of my bedroom window, searching for
Reminiscence of summer
Looking outside, remembering the luscious green leaves
The open space of dewdrop grass
Now is filled with a carpet of rustic leaves
The trees filled with bouquets of burnt brown and red leaves,
I wondered, maybe the children still played,
The cows still champed on the cud
Had these days of the sun plummeting on my back gone?

Lucy Karpinski (15)
St Gabriel's School, Newbury

HOMOPHOBIA

They walked down the street,
Looking at their feet,
Waiting for the first salvo of vicious comments.
They passed the bar,
Bracing themselves,
Gritting their teeth,
Clenching their fists,
Hand in hand.
Hand in hand they stared,
Gazing into their reflection.
They saw themselves for who they were,
Not for what they did.
For who they were,
Two men.

Rosie Bell (14)
St Gabriel's School, Newbury

THE DOLPHIN

Glistening
Glimmering
Leaping through the air

Silently
Slumbering
As if they are not there

Wonderful
Worshipping
They do not care

Beautiful
Bountiful
They come from where?

Magically
Majestically
Kill them if you dare.

Alice Staker (11)
St Gabriel's School, Newbury

WINTER'S WAY

Winter whined
through the glistening stream
then uttered a long
piercing scream

Winter hid
behind the snow-white trees
her hair soft
and cold bitten knees

Winter whipped
along the rustling ground
taking little children's mittens
and getting lost in the crowd.

Pippa Boyd (13)
St Gabriel's School, Newbury

DEATH OF AN ELEPHANT

Dear, faithful diary,
I write of yesterday,
When the African sun
Shone down on me,
In a melancholy way.

My eyes were bright and glistening,
My pupils, round and wide,
Reflecting stars,
And Mother Moon,
A cloud-veiled silver bride.

I'm with those things no longer,
I'm in a better place,
I look upon
The sun that shone,
Across my wrinkled face.

Cry not for me my child
Your mother still lives on,
She's not in pain
You weep in vain
I'm with you, though I'm gone.

Charlotte Ashwell (14)
St Gabriel's School, Newbury

Fear

Fear is when you realise that they don't love you anymore.
Fear is when you're little and there is a monster under your bed.
Fear is when you're alone for the first time.
Fear is when you see your life flash before your eyes.
Fear is when you hear that tone in a hospital.

Fear is when you can't breathe.
Fear is when you know something you shouldn't.
Fear is when you hear footsteps in a deserted house.
Fear is when you don't know the answer.
Fear is when you don't do your homework.

Fear is when you are trapped inside a body.
Fear is when you get a telegram from the army.
Fear is when your parents go to court
Fighting against each other.
Fear is when you've got a price on your head.
Fear is when you're unemployed and there's a bill in the post.

Fear is when you find out who your real friends are.
Fear is when you don't get that one and only dream job.
Fear is when you hear the words 'World War III' on the news.
Fear is when you hear the life support machine.
Fear is when it stops.

Vicky Clarke (13)
St Gabriel's School, Newbury

The Secret Garden

The leather touch of the rose's petal,
The rustic look of the old bench's metal,
The sweet perfume of the honeysuckle,
The happy sound of the child's chuckle,
The wet touch of the dew-laid grass,
The wispy wind blowing past.

The rough touch of the brunette bark,
The true sound of the twittering lark,
The fresh smell of the immaculate air,
The glittering rainbow everywhere,
The fair garden will always stay
Hidden away from day to day.

Frances Norris (13)
St Gabriel's School, Newbury

MAGNIFICENT MOLE

I went to my window and there I saw
My cat and my dog lying together on the floor,
They were up to mischief, what a surprise,
You could see it written in their eyes.

Lying side by side upon the grass,
I wondered how long this could possibly last,
And then I saw the fresh mole hill,
Which made me stand incredibly still.

Then all of a sudden, the cat drew back to pounce
And the dog jumped up and began to bounce,
With his paws he started to dig,
And covered the cat with black earth and twigs.

The cat looked angry and stalked away,
Leaving the dog to continue to play,
As for the mole it had gone to ground,
It certainly wasn't going to hang around!

And since that time I've always liked moles,
Even if our gardener curses all their new holes,
They are so furry, soft and sweet,
Having one as a pet would be such a treat!

Catherine Ramsbottom (11)
St Gabriel's School, Newbury

I Was There

I was there that day as it happened,
Sitting at my desk,
Everyone confused.
What had happened?
Told to stay in our offices.
A fire in the other building!
Told to 'Get out now!'
A bomb in the other building!
Then it happened! The other plane hit!
All I knew was we had to escape.
I ran round all the offices on my floor,
Shouting, 'Get out now or you'll die!'
Down the stairs and out the door,
'We've made it!' someone cries.
All I can remember is shouting,
'Get out now or you'll die!'
So many made it, so why,
Oh why didn't I?

Emma Bates (13)
St Gabriel's School, Newbury

Chocolate

The beautiful bar what a sight
Lying alone in the dark dark night
Shining like a star
The purple wrapper glistens

The predator creeps down the stairs
Her head peeps round the kitchen door
There it lay all alone,
The predator could resist no more

She pounced on the defenceless bar
Ripped open the wrapper and gasped.
The brown squares drew her in
She snapped off a piece and popped it in.

The piece went in; it was incredible.
The milky taste went down her throat.
She snapped off another piece, then another
Gobbled down in a fraction of an hour
Put the wrapper in the bin and sidled back upstairs.

Hayley Stalker (12)
St Gabriel's School, Newbury

THE PUPPY

The brand new puppy
All small and cute
The cutest I've ever seen
And she's mine, all mine I thought.
I saw her in the pet shop
Just down the road.
We weren't supposed to buy one
We were only looking
But there she was
So cute and cuddly.
We asked the man
If we could hold her
All soft and fluffy with bright blue eyes
Looking up at me with lots of love
Yes lots of love
That day she was mine, all mine!

Emily McMullin (12)
St Gabriel's School, Newbury

The Shark

The deep, blue, murky sea,
Where tropical fish swim lazily,
A huge, enormous, slick body moves swiftly
With only a four-letter word on its mind,
'Food'
With a flick of the tail and snap of the jaws
I'm not surprised he doesn't have fur and claws,
Now all my friends you shall see how wicked and cruel sharks can be,
The small, tiny seal never saw the light of day,
Before the horrid thing took its life away . . .
Now will you think differently about swimming far out to sea?

Lorna Fisher (12)
St Gabriel's School, Newbury

My Grandad

Sitting in his favourite chair,
bored, like a lion waiting for his next meal.
Then looks at his newspaper
and then delicately picks up his pen
and starts his crossword.
He taps his head in wonder,
thinking of difficult clues.
His mind ticking
like an unexploded bomb.
Suddenly he smiles angelically,
as he scrawls his answer down.

Charlotte Rogers (12)
St Gabriel's School, Newbury

LONELINESS

Rushing to school just in case
Someone's decided to be my friend.
I tell my mum,
She tried to help.
'Try harder' echoes in my ears.
I reach the playground and slip along.
The day ahead looks bleak.
With no one's ear to whisper in,
It seems the joke's on me.

I try to smile,
My face refuses.
I'm even at war with myself.
So my days go on silent and bare.
With no one to talk to
And no one who cares.

Nuala Williams (12)
St Gabriel's School, Newbury

AUTUMN LEAVES

Being blown about,
The leaves float down.
Twisting and turning round and round.
The leaves turn a colourful red, bronze, yellow and brown.
Falling gently onto the ground,
The leaves get picked up by the wind.
Put to sleep in a pile,
They rot into compost ready for another day.

Becky Brown (11)
St Gabriel's School, Newbury

TIME

The world never stops ticking
As time ticks by
The world keeps spinning
Clouds move in the sky
Planets orbit around the sun
Owls howl at night
The sun shines every day
Birds take flight
People don't stop breathing
Grass is always green
Clock hands never stop ticking
Lizards are never seen
Lions are always the loudest
Mice can rarely be heard
The fox will always eat hare
Elephants live in a herd
The past cannot be changed
It is always set in stone
If you're together, you're together
If you're alone, you're alone.

Laura Harradine-Greene (12)
St Gabriel's School, Newbury

MY ROOM

I sleep in a cupboard,
Or that's how it seems,
Just 11 by 9,
To hold all my dreams!

Bright green walls,
Make it my special place,
But nowhere to put things,
Not enough space!

Never quite tidy,
Never pristine,
But this is my room,
Never been clean!

Beth Tilley (12)
St Gabriel's School, Newbury

POLAR BEARS

Winter
Sleeps in slumber deep
Still as fallen snow
Making no noise
As quiet as a mouse

Spring
Awakes to the world
Catching seals to eat
Capturing more throughout the year
After a long sleep

Summer
Watches the golden sun rise
Over the cliffs
Getting hot and sweaty
Cooling down in the water

Autumn
Keeps himself cool
Begins filling his stomach
He settles down to sleep
It's getting cold; winter is approaching.

Jade Luckett (11)
St Gabriel's School, Newbury

ARE YOU EVER

Are you ever
Scared in the night?
Are you ever
Given a fright?
Things can be scary,
Because they go bump,
So do those things make
Your heart quickly pump?

When you are scared
And need a friend,
Who do you turn to?
Does it depend?
What do you do?
What do you say?
When the last thing you want
Is to go out and play.

How do you do it?
How do you go?
Your mum is the one
You're sure that you know.
You sit on her knee,
And hold her hand,
You tell her your troubles,
And go to dreamland.

Siân Davey (11)
St Gabriel's School, Newbury

A MARKET

The jabbering voices,
The haggling voices,
The worried voices,
The pleased voices,
The excited voices,
The chattering voices,
The sound of
The market...

The scuffling of feet,
The waddling of feet,
The striding of feet,
The plodding of feet,
The shuffling of feet,
The stomping of feet,
The sound of
The market...

The crying of the children,
The shouting of the children,
The fidgeting of the children,
The screaming of the children,
The jabber of the children,
The mutter of the children,
The sound of
The market...

Beth Robertson (12)
St Gabriel's School, Newbury

THE CHANGES OF AUTUMN

The leaves crunched beneath my feet,
And in the fields, the sheep bleat.
Wild geese forming alphabets in the sky,
Fly over the sun, as they pass by.
And in the evening, the scuttling sound
Of mice and voles, retreating underground.

And like an aurora, an amazing sight,
On the thirty-first day, the Hallowe'en night,
The witches and devils knocking on a door,
Asking for treats, and then they want more.
As people party, the music booms,
Under the gleam of the round full moon.

As the days wear on, cold attacks your hand,
Like a magician casting spells across the land,
And the merciless weather, which doesn't care,
Strips the trees, leaving them bare.
And frost attacks the fresh green grass,
As the land is engulfed in winter's tight grasp.

Abi Goulding (14)
St Gabriel's School, Newbury

11TH SEPTEMBER 2001

A usual sunny day, on a continent far away.
The clouds soft and glowing, no seep of darkness showing.
The constant chitter-chatter in the streets.
In cafeterias where people eat.

Grey shapes sailing through the sky, while black images fall.
The smudged eyes of people below, too devastated to look at it all.
Falling from the sky, their mouths open in sorrow.
Minds are dreading, what will bring tomorrow?

Emotions running wild, trapped in a room.
Faces looking, hoping it will all be over soon.
The sun setting under the black sheet of death.
People shouting, wailing, crying, for the tragedy to come and rest.

Alexandra Vevers (13)
St Gabriel's School, Newbury

GEMINI

G rowing together,
E ntertaining each other,
M inds thinking alike,
I magining the future,
N avigating our lives,
I ntrigued by what we see.

T he time has come to be apart,
W e have to turn away,
I n all my thoughts I
N ever thought I would have to be this way.

I n my mind I am filled with sorrow,
D estroying all the happy thoughts,
E nvisage a dark place,
N ever together again,
T urning to this new place,
I nvesting in my life ahead,
C ollege starts,
A nd I feel so alone,
L ost without my other half.

Victoria Wood (13)
St Gabriel's School, Newbury

WAR

Hunting, finding, destroying.
Disaster flies through the sky.
Despair grips the world.

Billowing smoke. Poisonous.
Gunfire, death and trenches.
Men hide in fear.
Children killed in cities.
Animals die through human fault.
Helpless and unknowing.

Dogs howling as rain turns to bombs
Fighting for evil, mud and flesh meet.
Fighting for good. And never part.

The Earth starved of the freedom to live.
Starved of happiness.
Innocent Earth in guilt-ridden war.
Peace will come
When death's job is done.

Jennifer Steele (14)
St Gabriel's School, Newbury

ONE STORMY NIGHT

One stormy night,
I was lying in my bed,
When the thunder suddenly crashed
Right above my head.

The windows started cracking,
And the door started creaking,
I was hiding in my covers,
And I wasn't keen on peeking.

The patter of the raindrops
Hitting the front door,
I had a funny feeling there was something
Crawling across my floor.

The gurgling of the plug hole,
Clogging up the drain,
It sends a huge shiver
Down my spine again.

Kerry Emery (12)
St Gabriel's School, Newbury

DIFFERENCES

I ran from the classroom,
Crying,
Burning tears of hatred.
Why was I treated as an outsider?
Different from them,
Alienated.
I was unique, a different colour skin,
But to them a dark blemish on a white community.
But can't they see?
It's the inside that counts.
I was born this way,
They would never understand,
I will never make a difference,
Always feeling as if I was,
The odd one out . . .

Jaishil Main (13)
St Gabriel's School, Newbury

Two Worlds

Trees rocking in the breeze,
Buzzing, buzzing of the bees,
Sunlight breaking through the clouds,
Get away from the crowds,
Just a big, empty space,
Birds above flying with grace,
Just a day passing by,
Just a day passing by.

Cars, cars, crashing, rushing,
Noise, noise, screams and shouts,
Rain slipping from the gutters,
Listening to those quiet mutters,
Seeing all the tortured faces,
Looking at the murder traces,
Just a day passing by,
Just a day passing by.

Natasha Perkins (13)
St Gabriel's School, Newbury

Alone

I've always been afraid to look you in the eye,
I've always been afraid to let you see me cry,
But yet I am alone, sad, scared and hurt.
My hopes, my dreams are fading,
Will I make it out alive or die here in the dirt?
And now life's little lesson is teaching me again.
If your heart and mind are battling your heart will always win.
I've always been afraid to look you in the eye,
I've always been afraid to let you see me cry.

Emily Osborne (14)
St Gabriel's School, Newbury

Willow On The Pond

The afternoon sun is blazing onto
The glistening, deep, sparkling, blue lake.
The pond reeds standing up as straight as soldiers
And the golden willow in the distance.
Its delicate branches finally touching
The cold, crystal water.
It stands looking into the fire of the sun,
Gently swaying in the wind.

Even though the wind prevails
The beautiful willow never fails
To stand with branches bent and bowed,
It never ever falls to the ground.

Rebecca Hilliard (14)
St Gabriel's School, Newbury

Sophie

Like a black panther,
She glides onto the stage,
Leaps across and into the spotlight.
The wisps of her brown hair tremble
As she stands proudly waiting,
Staring into thin air.
She suddenly springs into life
And prances back across the stage.
She is in the spotlight.
She loves the spotlight.

Charlotte Gent (13)
St Gabriel's School, Newbury

A Child's War

Mummy, why does that lady cry?
Walk on and she'll forget.
Mummy her tears are like knives on my skin,
Why does she cry?
She doesn't have to know yet.
Mummy look, she is crying,
Why Mummy, why does she cry?

Because her life has been
Torn to shreds, and all
She has ever lived for has
Been slaughtered by people
Too selfish and crazed
To respect human life
For its precious intensity.

Mummy can I help her?
Please can I help?
What are you, but
A mere child?
Mummy, she wants a hug,
But what has happened
To make her so sad?

I cannot tell you my baby
For your little face would
Crease in pain and frustration
An ocean would flow from your
Eyes and your life too would
Become a torment of guilt
Walk on, and you'll forget.

Zoe Hurst (13)
St Gabriel's School, Newbury

THE FAILURE

Always last, he never won
Would the habit ever change?
Never having any fun
He was just a failure.

He had no friends as such
Breaktime was his enemy
The teachers didn't like him much
He was just a failure.

He used to cry, weep all night
Scared that they would get him
He would shut his eyes tight
He was just a failure.

The library was his best place
Safe and quiet and all alone
No one he was forced to face
He was just a failure.

Among the books on the shelf
He saw a grey and lonely face
A reflection of himself
He was just a failure.

Soon all things began to change
Neither failures anymore
Greatest friends they became
He was now a winner.

Sarah Rossiter (14)
St Gabriel's School, Newbury

TWENTY PEOPLE

Twenty people,
That was all,
Wasn't me,
Not at all.

Twenty people,
Four planes,
Why now?
Why at all?

Twenty people,
Five thousand lives,
Why now?
Why at all?

Twenty people,
Millions of bombs,
Why now?
Why at all?

One house,
One bomb,
Why now?
Why at all?

Why me?
It wasn't me,
Not me,
Not at all.

Twenty people,
That was all,
Two countries,
One war.

Emma Nickson (13)
St Gabriel's School, Newbury

GENETIC ENGINEERING

Dad's a criminal
Mum's a shoplifter
What am I?

Dad's a Muslim
Mum's a Jew
What am I?

Dad's a blonde
Mum's a brunette
What am I?

Dad's a bisexual
Mum's a lesbian
What am I?

Dad's a house husband
Mum's a business woman
What am I?

Dad's a policeman
Mum's a junkie
What am I?

Dad's a teacher
Mum's a pupil
What am I?

Dad's white
Mum's black
What am I?

I am what I am
I choose what I am
And I am me.

Lizzy Hartigan (13)
St Gabriel's School, Newbury

MY GIRAFFE

My giraffe's fluorescent pink,
She wears blue pyjamas,
My giraffe has orange spots
And she eats green bananas.

My giraffe wears red perfume,
She sleeps upon a cloud,
My giraffe likes McDonald's
And she sits awake and proud.

My giraffe is very short,
She feels like candy cane,
My giraffe goes horse riding
And has a massive brain.

My giraffe lives on the ice,
Next to the burning fire,
My giraffe has fourteen legs
And I'm a great big liar.

Stephanie Poulson (12)
St Gabriel's School, Newbury

AUTUMN

Autumn whispered
through the leaves
over dustbins, in the trees,
cooling down the summer breeze
calling to the winter.

Autumn howled
round the houses
whipping leaves to the ground
weaving her way from green to brown
waiting for the winter.

Autumn quivered
on the water
preparing for the ice
waiting for that time to come
wishing for the winter.

Emily Pettman (12)
St Gabriel's School, Newbury

ENCOUNTER

She stood in the doorway,
Paralysed with fear.
The room turned deadly silent,
All eyes fixed on the figure who had entered.
She was a new girl.

She moved into the corner,
Whispers flying round the room,
Looking over their shoulder in turn
At the figure who had entered.
Her eyes filled with tears,
About to break loose.

They walked over to her,
Making the girl sink lower into the floor.
They took her crisps,
They stamped on her bag,
An interesting greeting.

Yesterday it was the coloured girl,
Tomorrow the fat.
They always succeed at their targets,
Too scared to stand up to the enemy.
Evil and discriminating.

Clare Weaver (14)
St Gabriel's School, Newbury

TERROR

The day was innocent, and so were the victims,
Both the target of vicious predators
Seeking only to destroy the meaning of the word peace,
As our perfect world was snatched from our grasp
All we could do was stare in horror at the picture of terror
And destruction painted before our eyes.
Twin brothers were slain by two mechanical birds of prey,
Evil raged devilishly in the scarlet flames burning within.
Clouds of suffocating dust rampaged
Through the streets of Manhattan like angry bulls.
The hysterical screams and tears of horrified bystanders
Were swallowed by thunderous crashes
As the most powerful city in the world crumbled before us.
We could do nothing as people threw themselves
From the falling towers clutching desperately to any hope of survival.
So why?
Why would anyone want to inflict such pain and heartache on others?
We can only wonder and hope it will not happen again . . .

Laura Fleming (13)
St Gabriel's School, Newbury

MY ROOM

If you come through the blue door,
And look upon the carpeted floor.
You will most probably see,
Things that resemble me.

Dirty clothes piled high,
When my mum sees them she will sigh.
Bits of rubbish that didn't make the bin,
Even John says this is a sin.

Mizz magazines lying around,
And what is that furry, strange mound?
They are of course my cuddly toys,
And on the wall various boys.

All the walls are black or red,
And there is James upon my bed.
And him being black and white,
I think my bedroom is quite a sight.

Rachel Liddiard (13)
St Gabriel's School, Newbury

HAUNTINGS

P ouring, splattering drops of rain,
I n scary, haunted yards,
S creaming children and barking Dane,
C hildren playing cards,
E mpty classrooms, standing, beating cane,
S hrieking ghostly figures by the windowpane.

L ying skeletons under stones,
E erie wind whistling through cracks,
O ther beasts moan and moan.

A nimals croak and squeak,
R unning through dusty floorboards,
I nsects and birds with crooked beaks,
E very minute passing with a clanging sword,
S top, quiet, no one there.

Lynette Masters (13)
St Gabriel's School, Newbury

A STORMY NIGHT

The thud of thunder
On a stormy night.
While the wind whistles,
Throw the bright light.

The patter of rain
On the rooftops.
While the windows clatter,
And the baby chatters.

The flash of the lightning
As it lightens up the sky.
The ladies run downstairs,
As the baby starts to cry.

The dog starts to howl
The cat starts to miaow.
Go back to bed everyone,
Or there won't be apple pie.

Sophie Kilduff (13)
St Gabriel's School, Newbury

LONELINESS

Nothing's to be heard,
A bleak silence fills the air.
The night-time's black and heavy,
The streets - desolate and bare.

I am trying to smile,
But I just can't strain.
I am aching for love,
Once again.

I feel at war with myself,
I'm now alone in a crowd.
I am anxious and afraid,
No one's ever around.

I don't know where to turn,
There's no one to go to for help.
Tears fill my eyes,
I'm lonely by myself.

Katie Meek (11)
St Gabriel's School, Newbury

THE STORM

Lightning crackling,
Thunder rattling,
Rain thrashing,
Branches lashing,
Wind howling,
Animals yowling,
Rivers gushing,
Mud slushing,
Leaves falling,
Children bawling,
Wind is dying,
No more crying,
What a riot,
Now it's quiet,
The storm is over,
Earth is sober.

Rebecca Le Flufy (11)
St Gabriel's School, Newbury

THE SONG OF THE SEA
(Dedicated to Esther Miller)

The swelling shores abound and then reside,
The moon rows on upon the waves in pride,
Her sceptered robe is mirrored in the abyss;
The ageless song comes forth to me from this.
A rushing wind within the poet's soul -
Obsidian in need to live, console.
The diamond glint of spectres on the shore,
Moaning down the hollows of bronze halls,
Hear the iron of great Charybdis' howl,
Where the breath of Shu about the crags does prowl.
Yet the ruby vein of Earth in dawning fire
Carries home in barques the fishers of desire.
Her sapphire smokes upon the rocks have burst,
Leaving silver crystals, quenching to man's thirst.
And in the myriad of golden haze,
Echoes of surf broke by ancient blades.
The cry of the eleventh hour that plea,
Where sinking hands outstretched have seen the quay.
And to those mounds of dust did watchers pray
For the safety of their love in jet-black days.
- See the turquoise and lapis lazuli hue! -
All sings the song which now I sing to you.
The chant that bids the stillness of the tide,
And brings us safe, my pilgrim, to the other side.

Anna Slack (17)
St Gabriel's School, Newbury

THE TIGER

Pounding paws beating through the thick jungle
He slows to a stop then lies down in the patchy sunlight
His striped tail twitches restlessly, swaying from side to side
His presence brings fear to animals because he is so fierce and strong

His eyes are big and brown as they stare into the undergrowth
Little cubs run out to him followed by their mother
The cubs climb over him playfully, prowling all around him and his
Desirable patterned coat that no man has ever dared to touch

He looks at them and realises that he needs to provide for them
So he sets off in search of prey and heads for the river
As he nears the riverbank he hears the sound of animals
He crouches down low and crawls into position ready to strike.

Mercilessly he attacks his prey and kills it within a second
In his mouth he drags it slowly back across the river
And lies it on the bank as he drinks thirstily
Suddenly, a shot, and he feels a stab of pain in his back

He grabs the meat and runs and runs through the jungle
At last he arrives back in his lair, blood dripping from his red chin
He drops the carcass and the family come over for their meal
His mate notices that there isn't only the buffalo's blood on him

With great concern she tries to clean his wounds
He is hurt very badly; there's not much they can do
So he lies down to sleep with his mate and cubs around him
Will he wake again?

Gemma Phillips (13)
St Gabriel's School, Newbury

HOME SWEET HOME

At the top of the stairs she stands listening,
Listening for the turn of the key

Standing there frozen like a shadow
Eyes glazed over like a dazed animal
She waits for him.

The thudding of footsteps, the muttering sound,
The shadow at the doorway blocking the moon.

The back of his hand, the bone of his knuckle
The leg of the chair

At the top of the stair she stands listening,
Listening for the turn of the key

The creaking of the door
The dull, writing eyes
The cruel, quavering mouth

The wave of sickness, the hot breath on her neck
The twitching hand

The spinning room, the ever growing darkness,
The cold harsh floor

At the top of the stairs she stands beaten
Listening for the turn of the key.

Sarah Bailey (14)
St Gabriel's School, Newbury

MY ROOM

My room is;

a place of comfort
when I'm sad,

a place of security
when I'm alone,

a place of safety
where no one else is,

a place of cosiness -
is always there,

a place to rest
when I am tired,

a place to study
when I come home from school,

a place of happiness
when it's cold outside,

a place to dream
whenever I can,

a place of my own,
a part of me,
a place to grow up,
a place where I'm me.

Helen Warwick (12)
St Gabriel's School, Newbury

A Trilogy On The Life And Death Of A Loved One

The walk of life

I walk across the desert sand,
I walk down the shallow stream;
Each pebble is a shining gem,
Along the shallow stream.

I walk across the flow of love,
I walk down the life-long road,
Each step another day,
Climbing uphill all the way.

Somewhere

Oh, you touched my hand like velvet,
Then you touched my hand like stone,
And my hand reached out for yours,
But you're in a land, unknown.

Oh, I felt your heart like silk,
Then I felt your heart as air,
And my heart, it wept for yours,
But you're in a land, somewhere.

The death chant

Now look in the garden
And, in white stone,
You see a cross with roses on.

And you would not say:
'How pretty in the garden
How lovely at the door'

For in the earth I lie,
Without a thought at all,
For you took my life away.

And they would not say:
'How pretty in the garden,
Oh, how lovely at the door.'

Hazel Luck (12)
St Gabriel's School, Newbury

DECISIONS

I lay there listening, through the crack in the door,
Distant voices, I've heard them before.

Why do they blame me,
It wasn't my fault,
My eyes filled with sadness,
My brain with revolt.

It's my decision, it belongs to me,
I was there when it happened,
Leave me my baby.

Peer pressure took over,
I'm young and unharmed,
He held me so tightly,
Calm in his arms.

Why won't they listen,
It's all up to me,
Do they really believe,
I can't handle my baby?

Ellie Cleaver (13)
St Gabriel's School, Newbury

My Mediterranean Island

The loud sway and whisper of the sea breeze,
In the lonely shadows of the trees.
The muffled ripple and trickle of a mountain stream.
If only I had a boat, I dream.

Here I am stuck in an ancient church, with only the
clanging rocking bells to comfort me.

They echo through the tiny towers,
And out onto the calm and wavy sea.

Someday I hope to be rescued from the chirp and tweet
of the bird.
Banished to this sunset island because of some ancient
drowning words.

Here on my Mediterranean island I stay,
Carefully, listening, life wasting away.

Verity King (12)
St Gabriel's School, Newbury

The Smoker

A single stick is burning,
It's grabbing you so tight.
It wants you to stay forever,
You're convinced that you just might.
It squeezes up your lungs,
It ties them in a knot.
It'll take you to a coffin,
And leave you there to rot.

That cigarette is *death*.

Sarah Duggan (11)
St Gabriel's School, Newbury

MY DAD

Standing in the river
In complete silence
Looking like a tree
He grasps his black rod
Flings the line into the fast river
Optimistically hoping
A twenty pound salmon
Might snap at his line
Time passes. His eyes remain
Fixated on the water.
Then if he has no luck
He changes his fly
And starts all over again.

Eilidh Totten (12)
St Gabriel's School, Newbury

MIDNIGHT

Horse galloping frightened through the wood.
Galloping faster and faster.
Its mane battering against its silky black coat
Galloping faster and faster.
Camouflaged by the midnight sky
Galloping faster and faster.
Its only light is the misty moonlit sky
Galloping faster and faster
And then into an endless trot.

Nicola London (11)
St Gabriel's School, Newbury

STORM

I stood face on,
The rain slapped me in the face,
Bitingly cold.
Great oceans poured down on me,
Like a bath plug being opened,
From the heavens above.
Tossing me, and turning me,
I was battered this way and that,
Like a feather in the storm.
Sheets and torrents of rain,
Spiralling round in the wind,
Till they splattered, and drenched,
The thirst quenching ground.

Helen Markides (13)
St Gabriel's School, Newbury

DEATH!

Death is with you all the time,
Loving it when you cry.
Havoc, mayhem it's his cause.
When you yell with anger
It's his applause.
Racing round us,
Hissing in an ear,
When you hear the deadly whisper,
You know the end is near.
You pace the streets, you start to run,
Then crash, bang, wallop . . .
You're done!

Holly Woodhead (11)
St Gabriel's School, Newbury

WINTER

Winter is cold but it's happy
children are laughing because
Santa is coming.
Snowflakes falling people
building snowmen, having snowball fights
Christmas trees being decorated
and families coming together for the season.
Decorations are being put up
presents being bought and wrapped.
Everyone eating big Christmas dinners.
Paper hats from crackers are being worn.

But is everyone having fun?
Is everyone laughing and
Playing with snow?

Kate Fields (15)
Sandhurst School

REFLECTIONS

What have I come to?
Is this me?
I look in the mirror, it is clear.
Glass reflects vision,
Of a face fresh and young.

I see a girl aged fifteen
Tears in her eyes,
But her presence serene.

Clare Beck (15)
Sandhurst School

DAY TURNS INTO NIGHT

The sun rises from the East to the West,
The mixture of colours uncovers the rest,
The golden sun and bright blue skies,
Not one cloud seen through their eyes.

The sun's reflection in the stream,
As smooth as what you've ever seen,
The stream's as cold, as cold as ice,
But ever so silent as day turns to night.

The sun goes down for night to reveal,
It's terror and darkness of all maidens' squeals,
There's nothing to see but the full moon's light,
Shining not day but only night.

There are millions of stars from light years away,
But still we can see them when we watch astray,
While we spin around the sun,
Our nights and days will always come.

Over and over and over again,
Until the world comes to an end.

Natalie Evans (15)
Sandhurst School

BONES

Your bones go click and crack
They can also snap
When broken in two
They can renew.

Off to the hospital we must go
For X-rays of the break must be shown
Wet bandages surrounded the break
It goes hard and feels great.

It takes six weeks before it's mended
Oh God, can't wait until it's tended
Look at my leg, it's white and thin
I can itch, scratch and swim.

I'm taking it easy for the next few months
My leg is weak and I can't run
As time passes I now realise
I must take care as bones are broken easy.

Alex Hughes (12)
Sandhurst School

POEM ABOUT SCHOOL

S   chool can be a pain, most of us go insane
over the thought of maths and English,

C   oz of all those numbers and words, drives us all crazy,
but worst of all we get to lunchtime,
then comes lazy Daisy.

H   orrible meals, dirty dishes, all get served to us
and if you haven't gathered yet she is horrible to us.

O   range potatoes, cabbage and broccoli that is our main meal,
and then come along the teachers and they get an amazing deal.

O   range carrots, a big portion of chips, and they always leave a few,
so in we go, we have a few, dip them in our stew.

L   unchtime end here comes history, oh what a misery,
all of this is just at one school, and that is my school.

Tyler Honey (12)
Sandhurst School

INNER THOUGHTS

I was once somebody like you, a mindless society-guided item.
Me, I long for something different something new, I found this,
I am no longer a follower, I am now a leader, in my mind's eye,
I am the greatest of the greats,
I am invincible,
A thousand emotions intoxicate your bloodstream,
The lack of clear vision makes me want to scream,
I don't know whether to laugh or to cry,
I feel so alienated I just want to die,
My pulse is racing I don't know what it is I'm facing,
The blue flashing light is a release,
It gives an inner peace for one second my thoughts
Become clear and those of happiness become fear,
I've lived my life in a day,
That's the price that I paid for drug abuse.

Rickie Cole (15)
Sandhurst School

MY FINAL RESTING PLACE

When I die put me in a coffin made of cardboard,
So that it won't last forever.
Plant a willow tree on top of me,
And watch it grow tall and strong.
It will be my tree,
My final resting place.
Although my body may be dead,
I will live on through my tree,
In every branch, every leaf.
I will feed it with my soul,
And my spirit it will hold.

Emma Wesley (12)
Sandhurst School

THE ZODIAC

Twelve signs make up the Zodiac
Each is a group of stars
Capricorn the goat is first
Sensible and hard working is he
Next comes Aquarius the water bearer
Brainy but also barmy!
Then comes Pisces the fish
Who is dreamy and unreliable
Aries the ram is next in line
Eager and always ambitious
Along comes Taurus a great big bull
A perfectionist who's very stubborn
The twins are next, Gemini
Both sides of them are talkative
Half way through comes Cancer the crab
Soft inside, tough outside loves being at home
In comes Leo the brave lion
As fearless and awkward as can be
Next comes Virgo the innocent virgin
Who's prim and proper and very obsessive
Then comes Libra a set of scales
Always fair minded and extremely charming
Along comes Scorpio with a sting in its tail
Very humble and forgiving
Last comes Sagittarius the hunter
They're always optimistic and bouncy
These are the signs of the Zodiac
As they change throughout the year.

Lucy Sedge (11)
Sandhurst School

MY DOG

Cindy is my dog's name
Who always wants to play a game
She is a very sweet doggy
But always comes in wet and soggy
She is always very sleepy
And sometimes can be weepy
But is really cute and cuddly
And very very bubbly
She'll always sit
For a biscuit
Then will be good all day
She dislikes cats
Along with rats
But I don't mind anyway
As she will just get on and play
Cindy is my dog's name
Who always wants to play a game.

Dee Wolfe (11)
Sandhurst School

MY DOG

If you can take orders from other people,
If you can be told off and not cry,
If you greet people and treat them the same,
If someone annoys you and you don't get angry,
If you can do things first time,
If you can keep your cool under pressure,
Then you're just like my dog.

Matthew Middlebrook (12)
Sandhurst School

THE BLUE PLANET

Freshwater lakes under the sea
Motionless sheets of blackness
Sulphurous creatures gorging on the stench of rotten eggs
Hunters with flashing lures attracting their prey
Like moths to a candle
Precious rubies, revealed by rouge light
Darting prey, cloaked in the colours of the ocean
Razor-like teeth slice through sapphire walls
The dead stripped clean to their bleached bones
Food for millions

Life on the blue planet.

Jemma Howard (12)
Sandhurst School

THE MONSTER UNDER LONDON

Here it comes,
I'll close my eyes,
It's no use,
I can still feel it,
The wind is on my face,
The monster is forever approaching,
It's getting closer and closer,
The wind is so strong,
It's pushing me back,
I can see its red and white eyes,
They get closer, closer, brighter, brighter and . . .
The train stops at the station.

Simon Amphlett (12)
Sandhurst School

BILLY

Billy was super
Billy was great
He was the coolest
He was my best mate.

Billy was a leader
Billy was the best
He led the school
With style and zest.

Billy was clever
Billy was smart
With bright blue eyes
And golden heart.

With mountains of strength
And a shoulder to cry on
He was perfect
What a shame he's gone.

Matt Bull (12)
Sandhurst School

SCHOOL

At the beginning of the day,
In the middle of May,
School makes you feel down,
I'd rather be in town.

Whilst the teacher is moaning with fury,
I'd rather be in a jury,
I'd rather be with my nan,
Or better, with Dan.

School dinners are really down,
So I end up with a frown,
Now it is the end of the day,
I must go home and play.

Alan Roper (11)
Sandhurst School

THE WAR

Germans starting a war . . .
How much more will we score?
Mums and dads dying
And their children crying
How much more will we score?
Bullets thrusting
Metal rusting
How much more will we score
In the second world war?
Torpedoes whirling
Missiles twirling
How much more will we score?
Grenades throwing
Guns blowing
How much more will they score
In the second world war?
Bombs occurring
Germans are lurking
How much more will they score?
Houses explode
People erode
How much more will we score
In the second world war?

Tom Currie (11)
Sandhurst School

THE NIGHTS OF HALLOWE'EN

Hallowe'en, Hallowe'en, Hallowe'en,
is always filled with frights,
the monsters, ghouls and ghosts of Hallowe'en nights!

Piles of sweets and lots of treats
or maybe a trick or two,
is there someone ready and waiting
to jump out and shout at you *boo!*

Hollowed out pumpkins,
give off an eerie light,
one of many traditions on Hallowe'en nights!

Go outside, but beware my child,
of things that lurk out there,
things that jump out, scream and shout,
and give you quite a scare.

Going shopping for masks
that spook you on first sight,
one of the many joys of Hallowe'en nights!

Kids trick or treating,
out there on the street,
dressed in fiendish costumes,
of things you wouldn't like to meet.

Hallowe'en, Hallowe'en, Hallowe'en,
is always filled with frights,
the monsters, ghouls and ghost of Hallowe'en nights!

Adam Meadway (13)
Sandhurst School

MY LITTLE CAT

My little cat is black and white,
He sleeps all day and runs all night.
When I come home he's always there,
His favourite place is my mum's chair.

From the window sill so high,
He watches the world go by.
He flicks his tail at the sound of a bird,
And even when the dustman's heard.

When twilight comes and the sun goes down,
He loves to chase the insects round!
I call him Tig 'cause he's got Tiger stripes,
Paws so soft and eyes so bright.

Rachael Arnott (12)
Sandhurst School

THE BEACH

The beach is a place where people go to enjoy their holiday.
The beach is a place where you can swim.
The beach is a place where you can eat ice-cream.
The beach is a place where the sun is hot.
The beach is a place where you can get a tan.
The beach is a place where there is sand.
The beach is a place where there is blue sea.
The beach is a place where there is fresh air.
The beach is a place where people relax.
The beach is a place where you can go fishing.
The beach is a place where you can play and have fun.

Angelo Pascucci (11)
Sandhurst School

Rugby Union

R is for rough like a plank of wood
U is for unbeatable like our team
G is for grubby because that's what you look like
B is for ball like the egg shaped one
Y is for yikes it's coming my *wayyyy!*

U is for undaunted because we're not afraid
N is for nil not a score that we like
I   is for injury, oh not again
O is for operation on broken arms and legs
N is for noses all bloody and bent.

Nathan Mulliner (11)
Sandhurst School

Football

F   ootball is great.
O n the ball all the game.
O ne goal can win the game.
T   o the top we could go.
B   all goes to one end to another.
A   lways give one hundred per cent.
L   ose, win or draw.
L   ove it so much, it's the game I will always play.

Adam Mark Keen (14)
Sandhurst School

Footy Poem

Football's my craze
I'll play it with anybody, any place,
I want to play for the England team
That's my dream.

These are the teams that are the best
Reading, Barcelona, Manchester
And Inter
They're definitely better than the rest.

Christopher Roderick (11)
Sandhurst School

SANDHURST

S is for such a good school
A is for an opportunity to succeed
N is for neat and tidy
D is for don't be silly
H is for help at hand
U is for underachiever, not a word we have to use
R is for Romer, the *best* house in the school
S is for success
T is for tuck your shirt in!

Josh Scantlebury (11)
Sandhurst School

CHRISTMAS

C hristmas is here once again,
H oping to get the things I want.
R udolph is coming pulling Santa's sleigh,
I n my bed excited I lay.
S now is falling to the ground,
T onight I cannot get to sleep
M y excitement is just too much,
A ll my presents I cannot wait to see,
S itting under the Christmas tree.

Daniel Pigney (11)
Sandhurst School

HELP MISS, I'M STRUGGLING

'Help Miss, I'm struggling,'
Fingers, mind, calculator,
They all count, why can't I?

'Miss, can you help me please?'
Minus, quadrilateral, patterns,
What do they mean?

'I wish she'd listen,'
Subtractions, multiply, protractions,
It's mind boggling to me.

'Why don't you help me?'
Set square, right angle, divide,
My mind's going to blow.

'Miss help me,'
Fractions, percentage, acute angle,
Why can't I understand?

'I give up!'

Matt Reynolds (11)
Sandhurst School

THE UNREAL WAR

Boom! Went the rifle,
The bullet piercing through his head,
The opponent stumbled to the ground,
Which was a sign that he was dead.

People diving behind walls,
People hiding behind one another,
People rolling from shelter to shelter,
As long as they get some cover.

Grenades lobbed into trenches,
Bombs hovering in the air,
Innocent people getting killed,
But that's if the pilot cared.

People scared,
People thinking it's insane,
But from my view, I knew,
It's just a computer game.

Matthew Vickers (11)
Sandhurst School

MY ANKLE

I've really hurt my ankle,
It's really very sore.
Even though I'm not moving it,
It's hurting more and more.

I've rested it and raised it,
And put on a cold compress.
But it's getting more swollen,
Not getting any less.

So it's off to Frimley Park,
This is really a great day!
They prod me and poke me,
And send me to X-ray.

They say it isn't broken,
And now I'm home again.
I've got a pair of crutches,
And a really bad sprain.

Kea Hinsley (12)
Sandhurst School

EMINEM

I'm Slim Shady's biggest fan,
I've even got the underground music that he did with Scam.
Some people laugh and some people make jokes,
Just 'cause I'm so serious about this one bloke.
I've got a home full of his posters and pictures too,
That's why I put his music on when I feel blue.
Slim Shady's so cute but that doesn't mean I'm gay,
He's a married man and married to Kim anyway.
I also call Slim; Eminem,
And Dre sounds good as a friend.
I watch him on MTV when I can,
When I do I blast it up 'cause he's my man.
My favourite song of Slim's is 'Bonny & Clyde'
Because every time I hear it I begin to slide.
I think Slim Shady's the best,
I've even got a tattoo with his name across my chest.
Marshal's a great guy,
If I had the chance I would want to say 'Hi.'

Lauren Hancy (14)
Sandhurst School

MUD WHOMPING

Cautiously edging towards the slippery slope,
Launch body down squelching, slimy, eggy mud slide.
Speed gathering until the chilling channel of water hits.
Icily, with enormous power.
Clamber through mushy suction, rotting stench
Creeping up nostrils, mud black as ink.
Reach top, mud in hair, up nose, in ears, between toes.
Launch again.

Zoe Ford (12)
Sandhurst School

THIS RUT

Day by day
I wake up in the morning
In some hapless search for inspiration

Week by week
I have to keep on learning
Try to find the door from this age-old rut

'... *four thirty before noon, he wakes up from a deep sleep
in a cold sweat, he's thinking of her and how this just isn't right,
how she'd be much better off if things were different,
if she'd just open her eyes ...*'

Month by month
I continue just yearning
To maybe find a way out of this rut

All the time
All the time there is on Earth
I have to wait to see if she wakes up

'... *and thus he continues, until finally she joins him,
and they are begun, it's great until she turns out to be someone else,
he must find her and the process repeats, only with different characters,
then ...*'

She is her
I must now apologise
I must deliver her from this old rut

Day by day
We wake up in the morning
In some hapless search for inspiration.

James Histed (16)
Sandhurst School

ZODIAC, SILVER STARS

Those sparkly stars at night,
Looking down from the sky,
Those future-telling Zodiacs
Are looking down tonight.

From the deep, blue
Ceiling of the Earth
They stare at us all at once,
Those future-telling Zodiacs and
Sparkly, silver stars.

They come to us, one by one, at night,
And all of them from above
Look at our homes,
Look at our streets, and look how we live,
Oh, those future-telling zodiacs and sparkly,
Silver stars.

Annie Ovcharenko (11)
Sandhurst School

THE WEATHER

The water cascading on my window pane
Tapping, clashing, running down the drain
The lightning rumbles by
Leaving heavy rain fall to die
Howling, whirling goes the wind passing by
Just to leave showers dry
The lightning flashes and then dies away
And leaves to fight another day.

Christopher Ibbitt (12)
Sandhurst School

My Favourite Things

Jellies and chocolate, liquorice and gum
A warm tickly feeling down deep in my tum
Horses and ponies, dogs, cats and mice
These are the things that I would call nice.

Shopping for clothes and spending my money
Laughing at jokes with my friends, we're so funny
Playing with friends on my scooter and bike
These are some more things that I really like.

TV and music, telephones and love
Climbing in the park, children below and above
My poem is finished, it's time for my bed
Why don't you think of your favourite things in your head?

Emma Elliott (11)
Sandhurst School

Prejudice

I'm not simple,
Stupid or slow,
I'm just crippled from the waist below,
Don't ignore me and talk over my head,
Please don't prejudice me
I'm not brain dead.
Don't push past me, cursing and bumping into my chair,
I don't want to be in it, life's not always fair.
An accident happened, changed my life one day,
A car smashed into me,
Left me in the road to lay.
Life is cruel don't take any risks,
You could end up a target of prejudice.

Tom Osborne (13)
Sandhurst School

SKATEBOARDING

I am ready to board
In my skateboarding clothes
Hoodies, skateboarding jeans and shoes.

At the top of the ramp
The thrill of excitement
Whoosh, as I speed I fly down
The sound of the wheels whizzing round.

The speed as I whiz back up
As I fly with a twist
A bang and a clang
As I connect back with the ramp.

Now I have the fear of falling over,
My arms outstretched and knees bent
I will keep my balance

Yes! As I go up the other side
To do my finishing trick!

Dean Charman (13)
Sandhurst School

MY POEM OF HALLOWE'EN!

October 31st is a chillin' night,
May send shivers of fright.
Werewolves come out at full moon
Beware of witches flying on brooms.

Magical mystical potions and spells
Be sure to check into a haunted hotel.
Evil laughing devils and howling ghosts
Will make you scream and shriek the most.

Mummies, awaken from the dead,
Sleep tight in the creaky bed.
May send shivers of fright,
October 31st is a chillin' night.

Suzanna Sanders (14)
Sandhurst School

FOOTBALL

I started playing football at the age of six,
I could do real neat headers and lots of tricks,
It was always my ambition and not just a dream,
To be picked from the squad to play for the team,

My big chance came when I was seven,
I thought I'd died and gone to Heaven,
The coach and manager came over to me,
And said 'Son, tell your mum we want your fee.'

Now it came true, my childhood thought,
And I could show off what I'd been taught,
The likes of Zola, Beckham and Wise,
A medal, a trophy or even a prize,

All these things were heading my way,
My skills were observed when I started to play,
My position was on the right wing,
Here we go, here we go, the crowd started to sing,

They egged me on and I nearly scored,
Then came the rain, it really poured,
The ref blew his whistle, the end of the game,
Jonny Fisk, one step closer to football fame.

Jonathan Fisk (14)
Sandhurst School

THE SKY AND ME

The sky is blue
My eyes are blue
My brother's room is also blue

When the sun comes out in
The blue, blue sky
It sparkles in the light

When I went to the beach
The water was sparkling blue
It reminded me of the blue blue sky
Shining in the sunny light

When I went under the ocean it was pure blue.
It looked like my eyes
When the dolphins flew
In the deep blue sea.

Emma Brown (12)
Sandhurst School

EMOTIONS

My fear is black,
It tastes like salty tears,
It feels like rain gently pouring over me.
My fear is dark.

Feeling happy is bright and colourful.
It tastes like strawberries and fruit berries.
It feels like warm sunshine in my hair.
Feeling happy smells like flowers.
Happy is bright.

Being angry is red,
It feels hot and fiery,
It tastes like peppers and chillies,
Being angry is red.

Karina Winslade (12)
Sandhurst School

TERRORIST ATTACK

On the 11th of September
Is a day *everyone* will remember
The terror that happened in New York . . .

Must dash, can't be late
Supposed to be at work by eight
'Goodbye my love, I'll see you later
Kiss the kids for me, I'll ring you later'

Arrived on time, so much to do
Where to start, don't have a clue
When suddenly *boom*, then panic sets in
It feels like the building is crumbling in

The force of the blast, the concrete, the rubble
I don't know what's happening
But I know we're in trouble

The building's collapsing, I've got to get out
Wherever I run to I can hear people shout
'I'll ring you later,' I must make that call
My heart stops beating as I fall, fall, fall

Shouldn't have dashed, should have been late
But had to be at work by eight.

Billy Stevens (11)
Sandhurst School

A Defender's View

Ice hockey is fast,
I have to be ready.

He skates towards me,
Teeth gritted with determination.
I hold my blue-line position,
Strong and firm,
I'll do my job.

Moving into the zone,
He winds up for a shot.

The crowd gasps,
Tension fills the air,
A goal, for sure.

The puck leaves his stick
But I am there, alert
I decide to block the shot
It hits my leg hard
Pain rushes down through my knee.

As fast as I can
I clear the puck out of the zone.

The danger is past,
The crowd cheers
Another one for the defence.

Sam Oakford (11)
Sandhurst School

ZODIAC

Capricorn the goat,
Aquarius the water,
Pisces the fish,
Aries the ram,
Taurus the bull,
Gemini the twins,
Cancer the crab,
Leo the lion,
Virgo the virgin,
Libra the scales,
Scorpio the scorpion,
Sagittarius the archer.

Taurus the bull
Strong and wild,
Leo the lion
Fierce and king
Of the jungle,
Libra the scales
Balanced and trusting,
Scorpio the scorpion
Harmful and sting
In the tail,
Cancer the crab
Pinchers and bright
So you better watch out!

Charlene Bailey (11)
Sandhurst School

LIFE

Morning has come the sunshine so bright,
Shining so much it was better than last night.
I look out the window the sky is so blue,
It was a nice day for me and for you.
Walking downstairs get ready for school,
As soon as it's finished I am heading to the pool.
But work to the best never let myself down,
Get the good feeling not messing around.
When I get home get ready to go out,
Have a good time, that's what it's about,
But when it is evening I settle at home,
'Do your homework now!' is what my mum moans.
Do it straight away then go brush my teeth
Get them sparkling clean from top to underneath.
Then slip into bed fall into deep sleep,
Thinking ahead what I'll be doing next week.

Jason Amos (13)
Sandhurst School

AUTUMN TIME

Autumn time the leaves go yellow,
Hear the children play and bellow,
In the autumn, the winds blow strong,
Christmas time won't be long,
The hedgehogs rummage in the crispy leaves,
The squirrels jump from tree to tree,
Put on your hats, gloves and boots
And go for a walk in the woods,
As I walk through the crispy crunchy leaves,
I look up to see, more leaves are falling from the trees.

Sophie Chandler-Smith (15)
Sandhurst School

WAR

People dying and there's nothing we can do,
It could be your family, it could be you.

Crying and screaming all around,
Bombs exploding as they hit the ground,
Losing your friends and seeing them die,
Families never want to say goodbye,
Soldiers leaving by the load,
Corpses lying on the road.

People dying and there's nothing we can do,
It could be your family, it could be you.

Lisa Hench (15)
Sandhurst School

MY NAN
(In memory of my nan Barbara Adlington)

When people die, they are always there,
Watching and caring.
My nan, full of love, peace and hope,
Will always be there to protect me.
I think about the love we shared,
And know that love's still true
Although I cannot see her,
It doesn't mean she's not there.
Wherever she is right now,
She's still my nan,
And I know we'll be together again,
Someday.

Laura Adlington (12)
Sandhurst School

Sports

S is for squash, the power needed to hit the wall.
P is for pool, the cue hits the ball in the pot.
O is for the Olympics, all countries compete for Gold.
R is for rugby, the vicious game of tackling.
T is for tennis, Henman goes for Gold at the Davies cup.

David Charter (14)
Sandhurst School

Dance

D is for divas at the disco
A is for actions from everywhere
N is for noise out of the stereo
C is for clapping to the rhythm
E is for everlasting dancing with friends.

Natasha Sandy (11)
Sandhurst School

Stars

S tars shining down below
T elling us which way to go
A lways there to light the way
R eaching out until the night
S lowly dies and turns to day.

Lucy Davenport (15)
Sandhurst School

The Snowy Day

When I go outside
my breath turns to ice.
I trampled on the perfect ice white snow.

I let my dog out to run around
like a maniac in the snow
my dog was frozen like a chunk of ice.

I built a snowman with my brother
my hands were bright red
from the ice white snow.

Later I went in and sat around the fire
I had a cup of tea
and a biscuit with my family.

Robert Caruana (12)
Sandhurst School

Teachers

T eachers aren't ordinary people.
E ach one of them are slightly strange.
A ll teachers have a special aura,
C ould it be they're about to change?
H ow about an alien species
E very one of them in disguise!
R eally though, they're just trying to teach us
S top us from daydreaming
   and keep our heads out of the skies.

Kaylie Brace (13)
Sandhurst School

SCARY STORIES

Scary stories can be fun
but don't go crying to your mum
one by one as you leave the room
everyone hears *crash bang boom.*

As it turns dark outside
people start to scream and cry
do not worry
it's only a scary story.

As I read more and more
I think it's getting boring
out pops Dracula *ahahah*
ha ha ha ha.

Tara Woodhouse (12)
Sandhurst School

CHILDREN

C hildren are for holding
H ugging when they're sad
I n whatever circumstances
L ove them and care for them
D arling little children
R ead them bedtime stories
E very day they age
N urturing them every day.

Laura Andrews (14)
Sandhurst School

SUMMER FUN

Out in the bright summer sun,
I hear the children having fun.
Running, singing, dancing, playing,
The gleaming sun on the sunbathers laying.

With the clouds high in the sky,
And they're in the pool,
Then they hear their mother call,
'It's lunchtime children, don't fall.'

After lunch, it's time to fly,
That beautiful kite up in the sky.
Oh look at it, it's such a wonderful sight,
Flying at a dazzling height.

Emma Chandler-Smith (12)
Sandhurst School

CHRISTMAS

C hristmas is the time for giving
H appy Christmas everyone
R eindeer flying round at night
I t snows heavy it's so pretty
S ongs are sung on Christmas day
T urkey is what we eat on Christmas day
M istletoe is a nice decoration
A nd so is holly and tinsel too
S nowmen are built in snow.

Lucy Crabtree (8)
Sandhurst School

ZODIAC!

Zodiac, what does it mean?
Could it be the star signs foretelling our future
Or just a ride at Thorpe Park?
What does it mean?
Zodiac means what you want it to be
How you see it through your eyes
Whether it be a star sign or a ride.
I see Zodiac as the beholder of all star signs.
Capricorn the goat
Aquarius the water holder
Pisces the floppy fish
Aries the radical ram
Taurus the huge ball
Gemini two faced
Cancer the snappy crab
Leo the lion with courage
Virgo the virgin
Libra the scales equal
Scorpio with its deadly sting
Sagittarius the wild hunter
All of those magical creatures are Zodiac
So what does it mean?
Well you tell me!
For what I see it as is different from everyone else
So the question, what does it mean?
Only you can decide on that answer.

Tristie-Alice Handley (12)
Sandhurst School

TWO GIRLS ARE CRYING

Across the world
Two girls are crying,
Both wanting more
And tired of trying
The first girl wants a Barbie
She's had enough of playing with an old one!
And blames her dad for being mean;
She just wants to be part of the scene.
All through the night
The wanting burns away,
But through the day
The wanting burns bright.
Barbies are everywhere
Why is life so unfair?
The second girl wants something to eat
But is too weak, to place the blame.
Her mother weeps,
While her father hangs his head in shame.
All through the night
The wanting burns away,
But through the day
The wanting burns bright.
Food is everywhere
Why is life so unfair?

Across the world
Two girls are crying,
One's full of life
The other is dying!

Alex Elliott (12)
Sandhurst School

MY BROKEN HEART FOREVER

Here I am again, wondering if you're OK,
can't stop my troubled heart
because we're apart, so many miles away.
Can this be true, and can this be real,
how can I put into words just how I feel?
I never knew love could feel like this,
just from one tiny kiss,
our love was like a river peaceful and deep,
and our souls were like secrets we could never keep,
but when I look into your eyes,
I knew God must have spent a little more time on you.
I was just trying to figure out,
just if I could live without your warmth of your smile,
or your heart of a child that's so deep inside.
I never realised just what I had,
now I must live with my broken heart forever.

Sarah Farrant (15)
Sandhurst School

OPEN YOUR EYES

As I walk along the streets,
I see a man that walks alone,
Distant echo of people's feet,
He has no place to call his own.
A shot rings out from overhead,
An old man lies in an alleyway
Dead.
A little girl just stands there
And cries.

Stuart Armitage (14)
Sandhurst School

THE DEVIL'S EYE

The devil's eye approaches a victim
Winks once
Winks twice

A heavy breath strikes again
Blood-curdling scrams approach the darkness

Many victims don't survive when the nasty devil arrives

Holy water is your only hope, when the devil does approach

Run when you can, and never look back, scream if you want
As the Devil will strike back

The Devil's eye a nasty sight
If it winks once you will survive
If it winks twice it's time to *die!*

Katie Lowden (14)
Sandhurst School

DEATH

Death dates back since man was born,
If someone dies someone will mourn,
Nobody knows when they will die,
They just hope they will go to the sky,
But is there really a Heaven and Hell?
No one can really ever tell,
Is anyone going to Heaven or Hell?
No one can really ever tell.

Keir Boswell (12)
Sandhurst School

THE WAR

The war is starting, we will win.
The war is painful, many lives will be lost.
A lot of people have gone mad,
some are extremely sad.

Husbands, brothers and sons have gone to war,
women are worrying and children are scared.

Bombs flying, people falling,
shells dropping and planes crashing.
Will the nightmare ever end?
I hope a letter of peace they will send.

The one they call Hitler is in charge,
we all hope that he will be shot for his evil crimes
against the Jewish lot.

'Bang!' everyone celebrates now the Nazis are dead.
We all give the heroes of the war a great, big roar
and three cheers for them all -
hip hip hooray, hip hip hooray!

Calum Doherty (12)
Sandhurst School

THE STORM

The weatherman had said rain today
And the once white clouds turned gun metal grey
Raindrops rattled against window panes
As the old man walked down the country lane.

It's not too bad, the old man thought
If I really get a move on I won't get caught,
A few more yards and then I'm safe
But the clouds grew darker as he quickened his pace.

A flash of lightning and a crash of thunder
And his hasty plan was torn asunder
The rain powered down on his balding head
How he wished he had stayed at home in bed.

James Phillips (12)
Sandhurst School

FIGHTING BACK!

There once was a man called Bin Laden,
He was a very bad Afghanistanion,
Bomb the Twin Towers he said,
Or you shall be dead,
When training don't ruin my garden.

September 11th soon came,
The bombers took over the plane,
Passengers shout,
'Oh please let me out
'These men inside are insane.'

Ahead the Twin Towers soon called,
Bin Laden at home soon appalled,
Into the Towers they went,
The whole inside soon bent,
And the people were literally floored.

People were dead,
And money was lent,
To clear up this horrible mess,
Workers were called,
The injured were bored,
And the world's population was less.

Guillaume Evans (15)
Sandhurst School

THE SUN

The sun is hot.
Hot like boiling water,
It keeps us warm,
It keeps us dry,
We love the sun,
We hate the rain.

We love the sun,
We hate the rain,
It makes us red,
Red like a tomato.
It makes us brown,
Brown like freshly baked,
But we don't care.

We can't wait till summer,
When the sun is shining.
The sun makes us hot,
Hot like a cooker.

We can't stand winter,
We hate the rain.
When it comes down,
The rain makes us cold,
Cold like an ice cube.

We hate the rain
We love the sun.

Kirsty Clarke (13)
Sandhurst School

THE WORLD

I've been up
and over
around and
around, the
world seems
no different
not on any
ground.
Spain or Turkey
wherever you
are, it looks
no different
not even the
spas!
It looks bigger
than anything
but really it's
as small as
a house, you
could travel
the world even
if you were
a mouse.
When you get
back it feels
like home -
finally somewhere
I can properly
moan!

Alice Bolton (11)
Sandhurst School

GONE WITH THE WIND

Gone with the wind
I travel afar
Roaming across the land.

Many wondrous sights have I seen
To many lands have I been.
I have cross the plains of African sands
Have even entered the Holy Land.

Gone with the wind
I travel afar
Roaming across the land.

Many beautiful sights have I seen
To many places have I been.
Upon the fens of Scotland have I wandered
Yet never to feel my time have I squandered.

Gone with the wind
I travel afar
Roaming across the land.

Many strange sights have I seen
To many countries have I been.
Across a glacier have I walked
And in the forests, beast have I stalked.

Gone with the wind
I travel afar
Roaming across the land.

I have no home,
No shelter of stone,
I blow like a leaf in a storm
For I am gone in the wind.

Emily Dunford (16)
Sandhurst School

THE JOURNEY

The register is taken
We answer 'Yes Miss'
Then the bell rings.

My teacher said 'Take this register back.'
I walk slowly,
My adrenaline is rushing,
I start to sweat.

I reach the corridor,
I walk to one side,
Then suddenly someone shouts.

My teacher tells me to hurry up,
I start to build my confidence,
I walk at a normal pace,
I feel great!

I can do it,
I know I can,
'Let's do it' I think in my mind.

I reach the office,
I feel apprehensive,
I put the register back,
I've done it.

My mind starts to cheer,
My adrenaline slows down
I feel so proud of myself.

Ben Willoughby (12)
Sandhurst School

PEACE?

What's the world coming to?
Will there ever be peace again?
Thirty-six minutes of peace since 1945
The American terrorist attack
Thousands of people died on the 11th of September
All of them innocent.

The World Trade Centres
Both have fallen to their death
The New York skyline broken forever
Many lives have been lost through
The stupidity of human beings
Of human beings who believe so strongly about their beliefs
That they would be willing to die for them.

Peace would be the greatest thing
Can a world not bring peace for one day?
There was peace - once only for thirty-six minutes;
Barely even an hour.
For sixty-six years there has been thirty-six minutes
Of peace in the whole world.

Can't everyone shake hands and forget the past
But it's just not that easy is it?
To forget all of the troubles
You cannot just simply trust others who have been enemies
Would they smile again, hurt more innocent
I wish for anything but war
I wish for peace.

Gemma Elliott (15)
Sandhurst School

SCARRED FOR LIFE

I looked in the mirror
And stared at the face.
It wasn't me - it was a disgrace.

I went to sit down at the icy cold bed,
I called it my temporary coffin,
As I might as well be dead.

The room was depressing,
The walls chalky white,
And the curtains at the window would let in no light.

Then a visitor would look in, as they normally do,
They'd see my face, back away,
Because they didn't have a clue.

See my problem is I'm not like others,
And will never be again.
This all came down to an immature boy who decided
To play with a flame.

These memories I can remember,
Of when I stayed in a hospital place,
The experience was quite bewildering -
But so was losing my face.

My face is now scarred permanently,
And my life was a mess,
But I learnt to live life to the full,
And my life became the best!

Katherine Lewis (12)
Sandhurst School

ISLAND DREAM

If you need a place to get away
from everything that's bad,
lay back, relax and enjoy the
time in a dream that I once had.

The sand's piping hot and burns
your feet with every step you
take. And no one's here to spoil
this day or make you suffocate.

You just know your life is better
here lying on this beach. So
keep this memory safe inside
and use it when you have to hide.

Because when you wake up
from the ticking on your clock,
you'll be awake again in the
coldness and the pain of a life
that's driving you mentally insane.

Rose Bradshaw (16)
Sandhurst School

PLAYGROUND

When we pick teams in the playground
Whatever the game might be
There's always somebody left till last
And usually it's me

I stand there looking hopeful
And tapping myself on the chest
But the captains pick the others first
Starting, of course, with the best

Maybe if teams were sometimes picked
Starting with the worst
Once in his life a boy like me
Could end up being first!

Luke Florey (12)
Sandhurst School

A CHILD

A child's heart is so pure,
It beats with innocence,
The gift of generosity,
This makes a child loving.

A child's mind is full of imagination,
Its thoughts are the creation.
As dreams are the invention,
This helps to blossom intelligence.

A child's soul is so energetic,
Its wisdom is spirited,
As youth is lively,
Teaching the child the youth of play.

A child's feelings are sugar-coated,
With a centre of emotion,
The shell of uncertainty,
Brings the gift of sensitivity.

A child's determination is strong,
Its needs breed enthusiasm,
Driven by a will that's powerful,
Makes God's creation unbeatable.

Catherine Kilpin (12)
Sandhurst School

FIREWORKS

F izzing, cracking, screaming, shouting, fireworks create a very loud effect.
I ntensive sound makes the ground rumble.
R ockets scream high into the dark, gloomy sky,
E mitting showers of sparks that light up the night.
W orried pets run indoors.
O utstanding displays fill the sky with colour.
R oman candles spurt light into the air.
K ids gulp, putting their fingers tightly into their ears and revealing large smiles.
S pectators watch in awe as the last, biggest rocket finishes the display.

Jonathan Frampton (15)
Sandhurst School

ZODIAC

A is for Aires the male ram,
T is for Taurus the raging bull,
G is for Gemini the identical twins,
C is for Cancer the vicious crab,
L is for Leo the lion, king of his pride,
V is for Virgo the virgin lady,
L is for Libra the weighing scales,
S is for Scorpio the poisonous scorpion,
S is for Sagittarius half man half goat,
C is for Capricorn the big horned goat,
A is for Aquarius the water carrier,
P is for Pisces two little fish.

Sarah Charter (11)
Sandhurst School

ZODIAC

I was staring up at the stars,
The beautiful, glittery white specks in the sky,
The dark blue background like the ocean sea,
And the occasional flashing light of an aeroplane.
Whatever do star signs mean?
All I know is that I am Aquarius,
To me it's a mystery.

My birthday's in February,
It's kind of a good time,
It's usually in a half-term in February,
So I don't have to go to school,
Which makes it really, really cool!

Philip Jackson (12)
Sandhurst School

FOXES ARE THE BEST!

Foxes are the best
They're better than all the rest
They're clever and sly creatures
With loads of great features
Like the round black nose
And teeth sharper than a thorn of a rose
Their bright orange hair
Is normally jagged or smooth or fair
They have bright beady eyes
At night they look like fireflies
The foxes' paws leave a small trail
He drags his bright orange bushy tail
Badgers, bulls, even an ox
There is nothing better than my very own fox.

Daniel Barreiro (13)
Sandhurst School

AMERICA

This is my day as it starts
As the window begins to light
I take a dash to the trash and back again
My wife is up cooking
And the children are watching a program
About Rover the dog.

And then I step into my car
And start to drive oblivious of
What was about to happen
I get to my French café
And I start to work

I stop and look up at the Twin Towers
And in the corner of my eye
I see a plane fly out of the sky
And crash smack into the Twin Tower
One after another.

It was devastating
They fell like large giants
Weeping as they fell.

Miles Turner (12)
Sandhurst School

THE SEA MONSTER

The sea monster lives in the sea,
In the deepest corner of the deepest seas,
In the darkest corner of the darkest seas,
That is where its lair is.

The sea monster is a detestable sight,
Its scales are the sickest green,
Its claws and teeth are black and sharp,
And all are covered in slime.

If caught your fate is worse than death,
You will be taken to its lair,
While feeding you slime from its body,
It will eat small parts of you away.

Elliott Westrop (12)
Sandhurst School

DOES GOD EXIST?

Sometimes I ask myself
does God truly exist?
A few years ago I found out
he was just an illusion, when
my mother was struck down by arthritis.

Watching her suffer stirs anger inside,
waiting to be unearthed.
Sometimes I feel like she is dying,
with incurable beasts crawling up her veins.

As the hospital appointments flutter by
she now starts to feel better
during her long days of the year.
Soon her life will be normal again
and her hopes of money to help the family
will finally come true.

Watching her smile again is enough
to cheer up the grumpiest angels
and as the emotional scars flutter by in the wind
I now know she is going to be all right.

James Shamtally (12)
Sandhurst School

TRIALS

Up and about at seven o'clock
Down the garage and unlock.
Load the bike into the van.
Today I'll do well if I can.
At the track by half-past eight
It isn't now too long to wait.
Section one I've done a clean.
By section two I'm getting keen.
Clean on three and onto four.
Still I haven't picked up a score.
On to five I get a one.
Now an ace cannot be done.
Onto six and two to add,
For a novice that's not bad.
Seven clean and into eight,
A class win is on the plate.
Section nine I get a five,
Hope of a win are still alive.
Section ten will be the last,
I've done better than in the past.
I've gone around for a score of eight,
Back to the start can't be late.
All the scores are added up,
The least will go up for the cup.
'Shaun, you've won!' I hear them shout,
It's been a great day without a doubt.

Shaun Moseling (14)
Sandhurst School

SLAVE LIFE

I am a different colour,
All my skin is black,
I am but a simple slave,
I want my freedom back.

I've been captured from my homeland,
In my thoughts it's just not fair,
Should I carry on living,
Right now, I just don't care.

My master is a slave driver,
He works us all the day,
And what we receive now?
Nothing not even pay.

I've no company such as family,
I am a lonely man,
I can remember my homeland,
I'd got back there if I can.

My new name is Billy,
I'd prefer the name of Frank,
And my little house, so very small,
Is also rather rank.

I hate my life as a slave,
It drives me round the bend,
Now I sit here thinking,
I wish it would just end.

Ryan Gardiner (13)
Sandhurst School

THE SPOT

The spot on my face
is in the wrong place
It sits there all day
I poke it, but it still doesn't go away
People stare
I flare

First of all
my great downfall
another spot
and yet another, oh, what a lot
Oh man, nooo!
These spots are my greatest foe

My mum says that
'No more burgers dripping with fat
and no sweets
not even for a treat'
Fruit is the key
because it's good for me
Tea tree oil I've heard is the cure
to make my skin nice and pure.

Roger Goff (11)
Sandhurst School

FRIENDSHIP

If you're all alone and
You need a friend,
I will be there till the end.

I'll wipe your tears
From your face.
We'll walk away
To a sacred place.

Just hold my hand
And proudly we'll stand.
You'll always be my friend.
I will be there till the end.

And when I'm old and grey,
Guess where I'll be?
Right by your side,
Just you and me.

Lauren Dawes (15)
Sandhurst School

ZODIAC

First there's the sun
Hot as can be
Then there's Mercury
A planet without atmosphere
Then there's Venus
Hottest planet of them all
Then there's Earth
With rivers and seas
Then there's Mars
Driest of them all
Then here come Jupiter
The biggest planet of all
Followed by Saturn
The planet with lots of moons
Also followed by Uranus
Very cold and full of gases
Then finally Neptune.

Heather McManus (11)
Sandhurst School

THE TWIN TOWERS

What once was standing tall and proud,
Has now come crashing to the ground.
Beautiful buildings for all to see,
Have now been ruined for eternity.
Many people were inside the towers,
Lives were taken within the hours.
Rescue teams did fight the streets,
With mile high dust for them to greet.
Innocent people's lives were lost,
For this murder will be a cost.
Terrorists have caused so much distress,
But we can pull together and get out of this mess.

Heather McIntosh (13)
Sandhurst School

THE BOY

In the winter storm,
A mother moaned,
She'd lost her only son,

At three years old,
That boy laid cold,
A waste of a perfect child,

He'd learned to walk,
He'd learned to talk
And make his mum feel proud.

Now his mum's alone,
Sad and cold,
Her only son has gone.

Hayley Beard (15)
Sandhurst School

FAMILY OF STAR SIGNS

My star sign is Gemini, the sign of the twins.
I might be smiling for a moment, but frowning the next.

Hannah is Cancer, my sister's the crab,
Always eager to learn, not missing a thing.

Mother's a Libran, the sign of the scales,
Decisions, decisions, but justice prevails.

George Hayes (11)
Sandhurst School

HALLOWE'EN

Monsters, skeletons, pumpkins and witches,
These are the things that give you twitches,
Graveyards, sewers, coffins and basements,
Aren't the place to be,
Because on the 31st of October,
Everything is make-believe.

Emma Diprose (12)
Sandhurst School

ZODIAC

Stars float so very high
In the black velvety sky
They float high above you while you are asleep
Dreaming dreams and counting sheep
Capricorn, Scorpio, Gemini too
They live in the universe just like you.

Leah Worthington (12)
Sandhurst School

HALLOWE'EN

Again and again
Year after year
Here it comes
Hallowe'en is here
Out comes the candy
With all the kids it's handy
With all the costumes
And the paints
That's what they are, little saints!
All the witches
And the devils
They're all such little revels
Round each home
As they go
Collecting gifts
It's time to go home
All the sweets
Are gone in an hour
With all the wrappers
They make a tower
Time for bed
What a great night it's been
They can't wait for next year
They're all so keen.

Natasha McGregor (14)
Sandhurst School

LEAVES

The leaves are falling
Slowly to the ground
Twisting around
Falling into a mound.

The leaves cover the grass
Like a blanket on a bed
With warm and vibrant colours
Orange, brown, red.

Mikayla Field (13)
Sandhurst School

SHOCK, HORROR!

As I wake up,
I hear some feet,
I look all around,
What will I meet?

As small as a mouse,
I crawl on the floor,
What could it be?
What's behind that door?

It's my sister,
She's what's there,
God she's ugly,
It's hard to bear!

Help me God!
I think I'm dying,
It's as bad
As a baby crying.

As I push past her,
And run away,
I live to fight
Another day.

Ben Harrison (11)
Sandhurst School

HER LIFE

She wakes to her life wanting him, needing him, longing.
It's a long way as she's still a child.
They both lie in separate rooms,
Him with nothing, wanting.
Her with the world wasting.
Dreaming of a secret passion.
A life of love and laughter, that's not enough.
They cannot be together as the hatred on people's faces grows
with their love.
She has no one.
She is funny, she's bright, but the darkness of her memories
drowns her ways.
The fear in her eye conveys an existence worth nothing.
To people she's lonely and that's why she loves him,
that's all a front.
She figured it was an excuse if something went wrong.
Does he want her? she asks herself.
As she sleeps, her breathing pounds, louder and louder.
She's deafened by her screams as her soul wants to escape.
Why doesn't it?
If they can be together she'd be happy,
If not her smile would change to the sweet smell of flowers
growing over her grave.
She is no more.

Jo Gale (15)
Sandhurst School

THE HUNTER

Gracefully moving the cat purrs contentedly
Eyes wide and bright watching his prey
The victim creeps nervously along the floor
watching the cat.

Quiet and softly crawling along the floor he pounces
The black and long sleek body puts all its muscle into its kill
So proud yet so calm he walks back home
and falls into a nice, warm chair purring happily.

Amy Fisher (14)
Sandhurst School

KAYAKING

The smashing of waves
against my boat
makes my adrenaline run high
and puts my heart in my throat.

The sound of the waves pierces through the air
like a thunderstorm just about to break
I plunge through waves right over my head
thinking this one I'd never make.

As I draw closer and closer to the edge
my heart skips a beat
and as I roll over the top
my jaws drop to my feet.

As I free fall through the air
I think to myself why I do this
then the water reaches my boat
and I plunge into the deep, dark abyss.

I resurface exhausted and soaked
and make my way to the edge of the bay
I get out of my boat and drag it ashore
and then call it a day.

Callum MacDonald
Sandhurst School

My Dog

My dog has lovely golden hair
He loves to play with me
He's like another brother
As close as could be.

When I come home at 20 past 3
He's always there waiting for me
Tongue out, tail wagging
For a walk he is gagging.

Leo is my best friend
I love him with all my heart
The only time I don't
Is when he does a fart.

I've had Leo for a year
It seems like forever
I hope nothing happens to him
Never, never, never!

Luke Hathaway (12)
Sandhurst School

Chocolate Cake

Chocolate cake,
Chocolate cake,
It makes my tummy rumble and shake.
I have it in my lunch,
And have a piece at night to munch!

Amber Coneley (11)
Sandhurst School

THE NIGHTMARE WALK

The night is dark,
Soundless,
My heart is pounding,
Walking alone,
The lashing trees seem to beckon me
with their long scarred branches,
Scared and lonely,
Rustling wind in the background,
Empty streets,
My anxiety surrounds me
in a dark cloud,
I look out into the darkness
and see nothing but a deep
black hole.

Hannah O'Neill (13)
Sandhurst School

WEATHER

Weather changes all the time
Cold or hot , rain or shine
Freezing snow and icy rain
Sunny spells again and again
Whirling tornadoes spin through the sky
Thick, black clouds pass by
Thunder and lightning
Isn't it frightening?
But the best of all
Is when snow starts to fall!

Kelly Brown (11)
Sandhurst School

HOMELESS!

It's cold out here,
Frozen all my tears,
It's wet out here,
Dripping with rain and overtaken by fear,
It's smelly out here,
Kipping in leftover garbage chucked out by cafe,
It's lonely out here,
Drop me some change and you'll be giving me some happiness.

Ryan Brown (13)
Sandhurst School

FLOWING MANES OF HORSES

Two horses at the bottom of the field,
A Palomino and a dark bay,
Tiff, Ryumedd - a Welsh name,
Up they come galloping up the hill with their flowing manes of colour,
They come to us for apples and carrots, they see we have none,
Back down they go to the pond at the bottom of the field,
No more flowing manes, they are resting and drinking.

Emily Owles (11)
Sandhurst School

MY SHADOW

I have a little shadow that goes in and out with me,
And what can be the use of him is more than I can see.
He is very, very like me from heels up to head;
And I see him jump before me, when I jump into my bed.

Stephanie Whitcombe (11)
Sandhurst School

SVEN BETTER IN THE END

Before Christmas England looked out of the World Cup,
With no manager to get their spirits up.
England were looking for a new manager to be,
And Sven applied for the managerial job to see.

I didn't like Sven at heart,
Even though he had a great start.
I wanted an English manager for our team,
Like most of the time it has been.

England are just about to go through to the World Cup,
Their last hurdle left is Greece and if we win champagne they will sup.
Since the day a manager from Sweden called Sven,
Came to England and we've played ten out of ten.

Richard Amey (13)
Sandhurst School

HALLOWE'EN

Witches, broomsticks, cauldrons and hats
Vampires, blood, fangs and bats.
Lizards and wizards and magic wands,
And frogs and toads from the pond.
Ghosts and ghouls and goblins,
And making faces out of pumpkins
'Trick or treat' children everywhere will say
Evil spirits will enjoy their day
Skeletons' bones will rattle and shake,
Spirits in graveyards will soon awake
Altogether they make a perfect team
To mix it up on Hallowe'en.

Julie Wilson (12)
Sandhurst School

My Cat

I have a three-legged pussy cat,
He is getting very fat.
He walks around every day,
In a very peculiar way.
He sits on my lap every night,
And curls up very tight.
If he crunches at his food,
You know he is getting in a mood.
He attacks my feet,
And then turns very sweet.
He still uses his scratching post,
And even tries to eat my toast.
My little cat is only one year old,
And he curls up on my feet when he is cold.

Amy Dunford (13)
Sandhurst School

Smoking

What is the point of all this smoking?
Can't you see what it is provoking?
Smoking's a drug and drugs are not legal,
So why don't we make smoking illegal?
Smoking is messing with people's lives,
It is nearly as bad as a drinker that drives,
It makes people criminals just for a fag.
Like robbing, stealing and taking an old person's bag.
So I am telling you now to resist the temptation,
Or you may put your life into devastation.

Simon Mepham (13)
Sandhurst School

RACE CAR

Three, two, one, go, go !
They're off down the straight already,
And Thomson's leading,
With Reid closing in there
And oh no! He's lost it!
Reid is in the sand trap now,
Harvey's crashed behind,
With Leslie spinning out.
It's the final lap,
Jason Plato leads but
What's this, Reid?
He's in front but
He's lost it again!
Plato's at the chequered flag,
Winning a million!

Jonathan Moir (12)
Sandhurst School

MY GRAN

One rainy day
My gran came to stay
She said she would pay me
Because she's a nice lady
She would pay me for staying a day
She made me tea one day
I told her she couldn't stay
Unless she let me do it
She then said 'I love you
Now get to it.'

Chris Foskett (12)
Sandhurst School

THE SHERIDAN AND ASHLEY

I may have a different accent,
my skin maybe slightly brown,
people may shout abuse at me,
but that will never put me down.
I may not be Jewish,
I may not be Christened,
I may have white friends,
but they never listened.
I may be religious,
I may worship a God,
I may have my own life,
but to ignorant people that seems odd.
I may come from England,
I may come from Pakistan,
but people will always tell me,
to go back to my own land.
I'm just a normal person,
living in this world,
where whites are giving their opinion
and people like us can't he heard.

Patrice Lilly (13)
Sandhurst School

FAIR IS FOUL AND FOUL IS FAIR

Fair is foul and foul is fair
Your perfect world is no longer there
It is good to stand and stare
Is it bad to help or care
Your friends and family no longer love you
The underworld is who they belong to
Your wonderful world has been turned upside down.

Sheridon Harmsworth (13)
Sandhurst School

THE GRIM REAPER

He loves the dark
And scaring young children
He'll eat your soul
He'll ravage your flesh
He'll rip you apart
Mind and all
He'll drive you crazy
He'll drive you mad
He knows you're scared
He's the *Grim Reaper!*

He stalks you unnoticed
He hides in the shadows
He crawls along the floor
He lurks round the corridor
And up the stairs
He waits till it's safe
He waits till night
He's the *Grim Reaper!*

Christian Fahey (12)
Sandhurst School

MY SISTER

My sister cries in the middle of the night,
It's all so sudden it gives me a fright,
She runs around the house with her blanket,
And she looks so sweet in her football kit,
She has very small hands and feet,
Which compared to mine is very sweet,
Once she knocked my mouth and gave me a blister,
But that's okay, 'cos she's my sister!

Alex Koulouris (12)
Sandhurst School

WAR

They never said it
Officially
They never meant it
Really

They'll never admit it
They were wrong
They'll never forget what
They shouldn't have done

They attacked
Each other
Families destroyed
Brother against brother

They said it was
Religion
They said it was
One man

But some say what the war
Was about
Is simply
Human against *Man.*

Yvonne Dalton (13)
Sandhurst School

WHAT HAS THE WORLD COME TO?

What has the world come to?
People fighting,
Killing,
We need to do something!

We need to talk not fight,
We need to stop,
To listen
We need to help!

Sarah Wyatt (13)
Sandhurst School

DOLPHINS

In May I went on holiday,
to Mexico we went.

I stayed at the Reef Club
and there two weeks we spent.

The second week we went to swim with dolphins
and held on their dorsal fin.

We wore floats and flippers
before we went dippers!

They came to kiss us,
one nearly missed us!

They jumped the stick,
they were really quick.

They pushed us along,
they were really strong.

It made me so glad,
saying bye was so sad.

Alannah Smith (11)
Sandhurst School

OLD

What is it like to be old?
Is it great or do you get bored?
What's it like to be bald?
Will I like it or not?

Watching TV all day long,
Reading newspapers too,
You become forgetful and your hair goes grey,
How long have I got?

Why am I worrying,
I have 50 years,
To play and be active all day,
When I am old,
What shall I do then?

Mark Turton (13)
Sandhurst School

FRIENDS

Friends are like stars
You do not always see them
But you know they are always there
If they are best friends
You know that they care
Sometimes you can trust them
Sometimes you cannot
And if you have boyfriends
They can be quite hot.

Jamie-Lee O'Hara (12)
Sandhurst School

SEASONS

Spring starts, birds sing,
Leaves and trees live again.
Eggs hatch, animals appear,
Here is the beginning of a New Year.

Summer comes, children play,
Fresh air, warm weather.
Buying fans or finding shade,
People making lemonade.

Autumn appears, leaves are falling,
Here come the conkers and chestnuts.
Birds are nesting,
Now all people are resting.

Winter is *white!*

Jody Lees (11)
Sandhurst School

MY DOG

My dog always sleeps,
He is always excited when we meet.
He will always be on the floor,
Begging for food more and more.
But when I go to sleep,
He will beg for treats.
His name is Deef,
And hopefully he will turn,
Over a new leaf!

James Tidd (12)
Sandhurst School

SEASONS

Spring is the time of rebirth
Flowers blooming magical colours
The spring brings warm air,
The fresh smell of cut grass
The magical feeling of spring.

Summer brings hot air
The blazing hot sun
Sweat trickling down my forehead
The ground burning hot
Long summer days, I wish would never end.

Autumn brings leaves falling from the skies
Wonderful colours, red, orange and browns
The roads scattered with deadness
Piles upon piles of delicate colours
As the last leaf falls to the ground.

Winter's cold sharp air, that freezes everything
Harsh winds wiping my face
Cold snowflakes falling from heaven
A white blanket shimmering for miles
Delicate spider webs coated in gems.

Sarah-Louise Reed (13)
Sandhurst School

FASHION

There are hundreds of clothes, they mount up so high
That if you could count every star in the sky
From the heel of my back
To the model's little hat
There still will be even more clothes than that.

There are thousands of clothes, so many there be
That if you could count every drop in the sea
From the height of my boot
To the shoe so flat
There still will be even more clothes than that.

Penny Simpson (11)
Sandhurst School

DOWN IN A TRENCH

Down in a trench,
Oh, how I hate it here
I can feel the fear
Smell the air damp and miserable
I wish I could be invisible
I could run away, stop the pain,
Feel like a human once again
I could wash off the mud and cold
It's starting to make me feel so old
My body is falling apart
My feet and teeth are only a start
I just have to lie here wallowing in dirt
Just waiting for someone to jump over and get hurt
Every day I pray to go back home,
To never have to go away or be alone
Some people may not be so lucky.
All around people are ill and dying
Last night the war took my friend Brian,
Just one bullet is all it took
When I get home I will write a book
Let everyone know the pain we suffered
Again and again and again.

Carl Lavender (14)
Sandhurst School

RACING

Cars arrive for practice on the track,
They're moved from the line back,
On the way round they go in the pits,
Which is where they keep all the car bits.

The drivers start the next session,
Showing their profession,
This is where they get pole position
In good or bad weather conditions.

At last it is the race,
You can see the tension on their face,
They position the cars on the start line,
And if a false start, they may receive a fine.

The end is near,
Worthwhile are all the nerves and fear,
For if they come first,
Then the winning champagne will
                quench their thirst.

Martin Calvert (12)
Sandhurst School

I ONCE HAD A SNAKE!

I once had a snake
And it always tried to escape
He was all scaly and long
And his tank had a pong
But we still got along.

Lauren Floyd (11)
Sandhurst School

Voices

Voices can be heard in the wind
They say whatever they like
They always have a meaningful tone
And they can sing or drone.

Some are beautiful, others are not
I wish a lovely voice would come to me
Or at least hear one
So I would know I am not alone.

I wish I could hear once just once more
A comforting song that opens a door
I would be happy just once more
Without one I would fall to my knees on the floor.

One more voice so graceful and grand,
Even a voice from a famous band
The one conclusion that everyone can see
That a voice the I want for me.

Trumaine Odaranile (12)
Sandhurst School

School

S   chool is about meeting new people
C   oming to school every day
H   aving great fun
O   n activities we help each other
O   n school trips we stick together
L   earning together is such great fun.

Abigail Tyler (12)
Sandhurst School

Moving On

As I leave the safety of the juniors
And move on to the comprehensive
I'm in the jungle now
I am the tiny mouse
There are elephants
And tigers all around
I scurry
In and out
Trying to find my way
I squeak with fright
As the elephants slowly plod
And the tigers roar past me
I retreat to the safety of my hole
And dream of being
King of the jungle one day
Until that day
I will survive
As I learn the law of the jungle.

Lizzie Goodchild (11)
Sandhurst School

A Stormy Day

Rain running down the windowpane,
the wind blowing hard, sends leaves flying,
and singing through the trees, goes rustling and sighing,
as the storm approaches on this autumn day.

Dark clouds roll by,
on their wild journey across the sky.
The weathervane turns this way and that,
and the wind tugs hard at my waterproof hat,
as I rush for shelter and shield my eyes,
from the driving rain.

Days like this are not much fun.
I would rather be under a clear blue sky,
with gentle breezes that brush through my hair
and birds singing in the scented air,
as I relax in the tropical sun.

Sarah Hiscutt (12)
Sandhurst School

TENNIS

Forehands, backhands,
To and fro,
Swing them high
And swing them low.

Hit them low
For a drop shot,
Hit them high
For a lob shot.

Serve them hard
With all my might,
I won't lose now,
I put up a fight.

I win the match,
I've got a smile upon my face,
I think about the cup
And where it I shall place.

The flash of the camera,
The cheer of the crowd,
All the interviewers
Make me very proud.

Stephen King (11)
Sandhurst School

A Day In My School Life

It's seven o'clock
My alarm bell goes
I jump out of bed
And put on my clothes

It's school today
Isn't that great
Lots of learning
I just can't wait

I have maths with Mrs Jackson
Who teaches us fractions
And French with Mrs Perry
Who always seems merry

Then it's time for a break
To have some lunch
I see my mates
And have some fun.

Then it's back to class
To do some work
There's a lot to remember
My brain starts to hurt

The bell rings for home time
The same time every day
And I just can't wait for tomorrow
To do it all again . . . *not!*

Anna Middleton (12)
Sandhurst School

ZODIAC

From January until February,
Aquarius gives the power of water.

Following this is Pisces,
The fish free to roam the open sea.

Then March to April there's Aries,
The bold goat who eats grass.

Next it's Taurus the Bull,
He is powerful, but short-tempered.

May to June we're seeing double,
Gemini says two heads are better than one.

Then June to July has Cancer
Cancer the Crab who has adapted to land or sea.

Then there's Leo the Lion,
He hunts his prey and takes no prisoners.

August till September,
There is the beautiful mermaid Virgo.

Then Libra, the Scales of Justice,
Showing people their conscience.

Then September till November,
Evil Scorpio with a sting in the tail.

Then Sagittarius, the bold centaur,
Power of a horse, brains of a man.

Then, last but not least, over the New Year,
Capricorn the ram gives evil new fear.

Robbie Coomber (13)
Sandhurst School

JOSIE

Josie had a crocodile,
Thats skin was as green as leaves,
Then every time she went near him,
She began to sneeze.

She also had a little mouse,
That ran around like mad,
Then the croc went and stood on him,
Which made her very sad.

Then she went to get a bear,
Which was very big indeed,
She got it home and it ran away,
So she got a lead.

She decided to ring the zoo,
And told them the bear was lost
When they found him they called her back,
And said how much it would cost.

She went to the pet shop and gave them back,
And told them she'd prefer a bat,
They didn't have any in the store,
So she bought a cat.

That is the end of our little tale,
Let's just hope there's not a sale!

Sam Lord-Castle (12)
Sandhurst School

RAINING

Why does it rain in Britain
On every day of the year?
That drip, drip, drippin' of rain water
Is all we ever hear.

So when you're on holiday
In summer, autumn or spring
Think of Britain
Forever raining.

Andrew Barnes (13)
Sandhurst School

NEW YORK

The New York skyline is no longer there,
Lots of people stop and stare,
At the ruins they left behind,
Looking for companions they may never find.

People jumped out windows so high,
People falling from the sky,
Suffering people down below,
Devastated by that drastic show.

Over 5,000 people are no longer here,
We have to pray for those who fear,
About their loved ones who were killed,
Those Twin Towers were very filled.

All this damage caused in one hour,
Thinking about it turns my mouth sour,
How could those maniacs be so cruel,
Don't they have any hearts at all?

Lots of people are now dead,
Show respect and bow your head,
Think about what they went through,
Don't forget it could have been you.

Kayleigh Crew (12)
Sandhurst School

OUR SOLAR SYSTEM

Mercury's first, what can I say?
This planet's dead, ain't going there, no way
Venus is closer but oh, so hot
Do I want to go there, I think not
Earth is ours, home sweet home
Everyone here is free to roam
Mars is tiny and very red
The atmosphere would kill you dead
Mighty Jupiter, sixteen moons
Planet of dreams, land of doom
Saturn is large, surrounded by rings
Twenty-three moons ruling like kings
Uranus is next, full of gas
Who knows what else it has?
Mighty Neptune, God of the sea
It's so dark there, you can't even see
Tiny Pluto, small and cold
To go there you'd have to be bold
Solar means sun and ours is hot!
We all depend on it a lot
It's really a star, a ball of hot gas
But we all need exactly what it has.

Rachel Bell (12)
Sandhurst School

SCHOOL, SCHOOL

School, school may be cool.
School, school may not be cool.
School, school where is Paul?
Paul, Paul where are you?

Whatever the lesson,
Maths, English, science,
Will you like this secondary school?
Paul, Paul are you ready for school?
No, I'm not because it's not cool!

Jamie Robson (12)
Sandhurst School

COLD DIP

The beach is rocky,
The stones feel sharp
As I head towards the sea.
I stagger and stumble
Before I finally reach
The freezing water.
Toe by toe I slowly creep
Deeper and deeper.
My feet are sinking
Into the sand.
I start to lose my balance.
Each wave splashes further up my body,
My breath is taken away.
My legs tremble turning blue.
A huge wave crashes over my head;
It sweeps me along the shore,
Dragging me under.
Desperate for air, I thrash about
And finally find my feet.
My body is numb.
I'm getting out.

Andrew Walker (11)
Sandhurst School

I Was Lying In The Darkness

I was lying in the darkness,
When a thought soared into my mind,
If only I could fly like a bird and leave the world behind.

I was lying in the darkness
When a thought floated into my head
If only I was a fish and could cruise on miles ahead.

I was lying in the darkness
When a thought struck my brain
If only I was a doctor and could take away my patients' pain.

I was lying in the darkness
When I felt a slight sting,
If only I was a bee then honey I could bring.

I was lying in the darkness
When my teddy said to me,
'Shut up and get to sleep or take a book and read.'

Jade Freeman (12)
Sandhurst School

Friends

F riends are always there for you.
R ows do break out.
I gnorance causes arguments.
E veryone needs them.
N ever let go of a friend.
D on't forget friends are special.

Michelle Trowbridge (11)
Sandhurst School

THE SEASONS

Spring, a time of new life
With buds on the trees
And petals that flutter in the breeze.
The daffodils spring forth as winter moves north.

Summer days, hot and hazy,
Time moves by slow and lazy.
Busy bumblebee buzzing by,
Collecting pollen with the butterfly.

Autumn leaves cascade down
A multicoloured carpet, green, yellow, brown.
Flowers wither and die,
As the last rays of sun say goodbye.

Winter, bright and frosty, sparkling white,
Snow falling gently in the dead of night.
Birds searching vainly for food to keep warm,
Fluff up their feathers against the forthcoming storm.

Guillaume Klimczak (13)
Sandhurst School

FOOTBALL

F   un for the whole 90 minutes
O   ngoing through crowds of players
O   ff-the-line clearances are vital
T   errible tackles are the worst point of the game
B   ad tackle, referee says 'Free kick'
A   bout to shoot, will he go to the left or the right?
L   ining up to shoot at goal
L   inesman shows offside.

Matthew Alden (12)
Sandhurst School

THE SUN AND THE MOON

The hot sun sizzling away,
Give us light every day,
In the summer the sun stays out,
When we're playing we stay out even later.

The cold moon shining away,
Makes all the stars come out to play,
In the winter, the moon plays with the stars,
When we're tucked up in bed asleep,
                    the moon is playing.
The moon and the sun keep playing,
The stars and clouds keep bouncing,
The moon and stars are out,
The sun and clouds are out.

Caroline Jones (12)
Sandhurst School

NOTHING!

I screamed at her,
But she didn't listen.
She crossed the road
            Smash!
The car hit her quicker
Than I could think.
She screamed
I ran to her.
The car drove off.
I cried and knelt down to her side.
I checked to see if she was breathing.

            Nothing!

Katy Wesley (11)
Sandhurst School

WINTER'S DAY

It is a winter's day
I cannot go out to play
The rain falls and spoils the day!
Pitter-patter on the windows
Squelching of the drains
Trees moving to and fro
Leaves twirling, twisting, falling to the ground.
Roads all wet, glittering like giant eels.
Headlights beaming, wipers swaying
Oh when will I be playing?
Five bells ring so I stay in.
Now we stay in waiting for the Earth's
                            multicoloured ring
I wonder if there is a pot of gold?
The bells ring, so we begin to sing
For we can play again.

Jessica Gibson (12)
Sandhurst School

ZODIAC

Aries the ram, always has a plan,
Taurus the bull, is as stubborn as a mule,
Gemini the twins, do the most wonderful things,
Cancer the crab, always wants to grab,
Scorpio the Scorpion, his pincers are as sharp as pin,
Aquarius is water, he is an explorer,
Pisces the fish, he makes his wish.

Steven McKane (11)
Sandhurst School

THE CHELSEA POEM!

Chelsea, Chelsea,
are the best,
Chelsea, Chelsea,
better than the rest.
Chelsea, Chelsea,
are better than Man 'U',
Chelsea, Chelsea,
your team will be thrashed too!
Chelsea, Chelsea,
are the blues,
Chelsea, Chelsea,
never lose.
Chelsea, Chelsea,
always win,
Chelsea, Chelsea,
you are the team,
I support through thick and thin.
Chelsea, Chelsea,
win or lose,
Chelsea, Chelsea,
will always be *The Blues!*

Tom Cooper (11)
Sandhurst School

GUARDIAN ANGELS

Everyone has a guardian
angel of their own,
they will never leave you
so you're never alone.

They may not make your
wishes and dreams come true,
but no matter what,
they are a part of you.

Life doesn't come easy
that's why we need a guide,
everyone's not perfect but at least
you know you've tried.

Without a guardian angel,
we would be lost,
in our guardian angel we trust.

Natasha Gontier (12)
Sandhurst School

CAN YOU HEAR?

Can you hear the wind
brushing past your body?
Can you hear the thunder
it's very, very moody!

Can you see the lightning,
flashing in your eyes?
Can you see the black clouds
and hear people's cries.

Can you hear the thunder,
rumbling up above?
Can you hear the wind?
It's not to be loved.

Can you see the black clouds,
surrounding all around?
Can you see the lightning
making a loud sound?

Can you see or hear these things?

Danielle Davis (11)
Sandhurst School

MRS RIDGWAY

Mrs Ridgway is my teacher,
Bubbly and cheerful,
Mrs Ridgway is my teacher,
Kind as can be.

Mrs Ridgway is my teacher,
Caring and considerate.
Mrs Ridgway is my teacher,
Understanding is she.

Mrs Ridgway is my teacher,
With a polo on her neck,
Mrs Ridgway is my teacher,
Funny, happy every day.

Mrs Ridgway is my teacher,
America she is from,
Mrs Ridgway is my teacher,
Emotional is she.

Mrs Ridgway is my teacher,
Gentle as can be,
Mrs Ridgway is my teacher,
Stands out in the crowd.

Mrs Ridgway is my teacher,
Talkative and smart,
Mrs Ridgway is my teacher,
Gives me a smile every day.

Mrs Ridgway is my teacher,
Stands out very bold
Laughing with experience
With a smile like pure gold.

Leanne Sullivan (12)
Sandhurst School

Music

First comes pop
Gets you moving to the beat,
Dancing all night
Getting up on your feet.

Second comes rap
Gets ya grooving,
Rap is sure
To get the party moving.

Third R&B
Get that funky sound,
A load of this music
Will get you spinning around.

Music is fun
There's no bad stuff about it,
Fantastic sounds
We could not live without it!

Laura Cooper (11)
Sandhurst School

Friends

F riends are funny
R eliable and true with
I individual minds
E verlasting and
N ever bored of listening
D iscreet and
S incere is what makes a friend.

Katie Avery (11)
Sandhurst School

MUSIC

Music is fun
Once you hear pop, you can't *stop!*
It's brill, it's great.
I could listen to it all day
You could listen to it all day
You can dance to it.
Like a disco diva
Or you can just relax and listen.
If anybody ever asked me about music I would say,
'Music, it's fun, it's great
Once you hear pop, you can't *stop!'*

Kirsty Currier (11)
Sandhurst School

THE TREES

The trees, dead still,
They twitch a little,
The trees, dead still,
They hum a song,
The trees, dead still,
The trees do a little wave,
The trees, dead still,
They cringe in pain,
The trees, dead still,
They moult in sorrow,
The trees, dead still,
They turn a golden green,
The trees, dead still,
Then finally they turn an everlasting brown,
The trees, dead still,

Maxine Girard (11)
Sandhurst School

LOOK UP

At night we see,
The utmost beauty.
The white moon shining
While the stars are shooting.

The stars are twirling,
With all their stories
Whispering words
That have never been spoken.

Only will you hear their words
When you're blessed with eternal sleep.
Then you will know and understand
And we will hear your silent words.

The peace of the silence,
That can never be heard.
Unless the stars address you,
With the lights of darkness.

As the stars cross,
In the sky above,
Silently they're wishing
For your own fate.

Virgo, Taurus, Pisces too
All so different and yet all the same.
We come and we go,
But we will always end in the stars.

Leanne Ledger (12)
Sandhurst School

THROUGH THE EYES OF A TIGER

I watch my prey with suspense
Waiting for the time
Three, two, one, here I go
This one's going to be mine

I keep focused on the boar
Trying not to lose it.
Run like the wind, I say
I can't stop now, I can't quit.

I'm almost there
It's in my grasp
One more powerful stride
And it will gasp!

I sink my teeth into its flesh
Slicing through the meat.
Once I've finished with this fabulous food
I will rest in the afternoon heat!

The rest of the day is totally unplanned
Just doing nothing at all.
Listening to the sounds of the plains
The animals make their call.

Natalie Smart (12)
Sandhurst School

CHITTY CHITTY BANG BANG

Chitty chitty bang bang all day long,
Chitty chitty bang bang is its song,
Chitty chitty bang bang looks so sleek,
The opposite to the ancient Greeks!

Chitty chitty bang bang is so fast,
Chitty chitty bang bang with a big *blast!*
Chitty chitty bang bang, it can fly,
So you are the weakest link,

Goodbye!

Marcus Hau (11)
Sandhurst School

SEASONS

Summer, season of freedom
Children playing in the midday sun
Gentle breezes swaying the outspread trees
Relaxation, no worries, no ridges on
                the vast plain of summer.

Autumn, dying trees
Children back at school,
Leaves swooping down from above
Fields of gold, red, yellow, brown.

Winter, *brrrrr!*
Rain, sleet, snow
Christmas is coming
Warm fires comforting you.

Spring,
New beginnings
Trees blossoming in the April showers
Rain, sun, rain, sun
These are the seasons.

Daniel Clegg (12)
Sandhurst School

DISCO DIVA

Disco diva-ing all night long
In the flashing lights listening to songs
Singing, dancing and having fun
My favourite songs all in a run

The room was dark and it was hard to see
Who was dancing next to me
The air was thick and full of smoke
It made it hard not to choke

The lights still flashing it was time to go home
I wondered if I would be going alone
My dad pulled up outside the door
He said he had room for one more.

Liam O'Keeffe (11)
Sandhurst School

HARRY THE GOBLIN

Harry the goblin lives in a cave
He's grumpy and misley and rude but
This is how goblins behave.

Harry the goblin doesn't like to be seen
But you will surely know
Where he has been.

Harry the goblin is sly and stealthy
He's on the look-out for people
Who are wealthy.

At the end of every day,
Harry the goblin goes to sleep
In his cave.

Richard Inions (14)
Sandhurst School

THE ONE FOR ME

I gazed into your eyes
What did I see?
Just a stranger staring back at me.

Years together seemed so few
The love for you, I wish you knew.
Sharp edges now seemed so blunt
Always wishing I had the guts!

I knew together we'd be great
I couldn't let this love stop at an endless fate.
I had to make you realise,
My love for you is so true!

I looked into your eyes
What did I see?
A future shining back at me.

Chloe Soane (12)
Sandhurst School

THE MEDUSA OF OUR TIME

The tiny creature stumbles through the pitch-black night.
The assassin camouflaged ready to strike.
His prey unaware he is being stalked.
The predator lies dormant, ready and waiting
for the right time to pounce.
God's tiny creature knows its death is near
but when?
It stands frozen, as a gaping jaw of venom
lures it to its doom.

Matthew Hegarty (11)
Sandhurst School

THE RACE

On your marks
Get set, go
Run, run fast
Don't go slow.

Before the race
You must eat
Lots of veg
Plenty of meat.

When you are
As fit as a fiddle
You'll be in the lead
Not in the middle.

When you can see
The end of the race
You'll run so fast
You'll go red in the face.

Over the line
Keep in lane
Punch the air
You've won again!

Tom Ashton (11)
Sandhurst School

WINTER

I'm sitting watching the rain fall
Plip, plop, plip, plop
Dull, dark, dreary day.

Lightning screams, thunder shouts
Crash, bang, crash, bang.
There is no referee.

The wind howls like a wolf
Swish, whoosh, swish, whoosh.
Trees are torn to shreds.

But I don't care
I'm inside, warm and snug
Drinking hot chocolate,
Wrapped in my quilt.

Charlotte Goodwin (12)
Sandhurst School

SKATEBOARDING

I love my dangerous skateboarding,
Going down my hill,
But if you seem to miss your step,
It's the ultimate place to kill!

Going up a vert ramp,
It's like being like a bird,
But for the extremely faint-hearted,
You will find it's very absurd.

Attacking a dangerous grind,
Doing a 50-50,
You need a lot of skill,
Because it's very nifty.

Speeding down a highway,
Not a care in my mind,
But I'm very, very glad,
Of being a mastermind.

Daniel Buckler (11)
Sandhurst School

The Chinese Zodiac

The Chinese Zodiac
Consists of 12 animals
All with unique powers.

The *chicken* sends you flies
The *dragon* makes the fire
And the *monkey* makes you an animal

The *pig* is a blast
The *rabbit* is fast
And the *sheep* will make you a ghost

The *horse* is the healer
The *ox* is strength
And the *rat* will make you move if you can't

The *snake* is invisible
The *dog* is immortal
And the *tiger* will join all 12

This is the Chinese
Zodiac.

David Allistone (12)
Sandhurst School

Space

A big, black silent darkness
Full of millions of stars
A home for all nine planets
Jupiter, Venus and Mars

Who knows what lies beyond it
Life forms of all kinds
With little green like aliens
Which only exist in our minds

It's like a big, black, bottomless box
Which squeezes in everything it can see
With stars and planets, people too
Including you and me

It's one of many mysteries
Which has gone on and on
But we better make the most of it
Because one day it might be gone . . .

Rebekah McVittie (11)
Sandhurst School

MY FRIENDS AND I

I have very many friends,
I hope our friendship will never end.
We play together all the time,
I truly like these friends of mine.
Lorna is my best friend by far,
But I can only see her by car.
She lives just too far away,
But it's fun when she comes to stay.
We've known each other all our lives,
We've never told any fibs or lies.
My newest friend of all's Rebekah,
I wish I could have known her better.
Another friend is Charlotte,
She's one of the best friends I've got.
Yet another friend is Stephanie,
She began school in the same class as me.
In fact, my friends are really cool,
Whether at home or at school.

Ellen Whalley (11)
Sandhurst School

THE STORM

Crash! The mighty waves smashed against the slimy, slippery rocks.
Dark gloomy clouds raced by faster and faster.
The bright moon shone down on the almighty sea.

In the distance a small fishing boat was bobbing about.
Suddenly a huge wave hit it and it was gone.
I looked on in horror.

As the waves drew in I noticed the half-eaten sandcastles,
Which were made by happy children during the day,
Now they would be ruined by this terrible storm.
Walking away from the scene I saw soggy, wet sand, pebbles
                                              and glistening shells.

Lorna Glazier (11)
Sandhurst School

LIFE IS GREAT!

L   Is for loving and kindness each day.
I   Is for intelligence you need all the way
F   Is for fun, you can't live without.
E   Is for excellence, there is no doubt.

I   Is for information we all need.
S   is for success we want indeed.

G   Is for giving up your own time.
R   Is for receiving a gift that is mine.
E   Is for everlasting joy to the end.
A   Is for always being my friend.
T   Is for this life that is great and for
    this life you cannot hate.

Rebecca Taylor (11)
Sandhurst School

The Strange Man

On my way to school, I see a strange house
It has plants growing all over it
There is rubbish everywhere
The house looks unlived in
Suddenly a light flicks on, I can see an old man
I think it is a tramp who has broken in
There is something different about his clothes and the way he looks
He has seen me and he starts staring at me
He starts walking nearer to the window
As if by magic, he walks through the window
How did that happen, I wonder, the window was shut.
He approaches me, I look at him
He is old and has a sad look on his face
A blinding white light appears around the man
I shut my eyes, when I open then again, he is gone!

Fern O'Guynn (11)
Sandhurst School

The Best Day On The Earth

The best day on the Earth
will be when the world can cry,
'We are all at peace.'
So let nobody die,
no killers roam the street at night,
no enemies to shoot or fight,
no blackmail, death notes or pub brawls,
no attacks or cruelty to animals.
But wherever you go, you will sadly find,
before you get peace, you must destroy mankind.

Roxanne McVittie (11)
Sandhurst School

Rain

When the rain beats down,
The wind is high
And the clouds storm across the empty sky.

The explosions on your window
Make you feel dull,
And the sound that echoes through your ears,
                  soon becomes a drawl.

Puddles try to conquer the road,
And stop the cars whizzing by,
Like butter over bobbly toast,
                  but all they can do is cry.

But all they can do is cry.

Hayley Thair (12)
Sandhurst School

Autumn

Every year autumn comes,
Leaves are falling from up above
Golden, orange, red and yellow
All fall down upon the meadow.

All the daddies use their brooms
To sweep them up, zoom, zoom, zoom!
This seems to be an endless task
'Can I play?' I dare not ask!

Now that autumn's gone away
The Snow Queen will come out to play
When the north wind does blow,
We guarantee there will be snow!

Sophie Heffernan (12)
Sandhurst School

THE ALLITERATION ALPHABET

Airy angels appeared above
Beautiful bunnies burrowed below
Crazy cats clambered and crept
Destructive dogs dipped and dived
Enormous elephants eat even emus!
Flying fish float and fly freely
Greedy Geese gabble and gobble
Hysterical hyenas hunt horses
Igloo insurance is inexpensive
Jumping jackals jab jaguars
Kamikaze kangaroos karate kick enemies
Lagging landlords lap lager
Minute mice make mischief
Nasty nits nip near necks
Organised ostriches often obey
Polite people produce payments
Qualified quartets create queues
Rodents and reptiles, rats and rabbits
Soggy socks - stinky and smelly
Terrible timetables - troubled teenagers!
Unethical umpires usually unite
Vicious vegetarians - vile and vivid
Wacky waiters wade in water
Xylophones - excellent Xmas presents
Yummy yellow yoghurts? - Yuk!
Zany zodiacs zip and zoom.

James Lowden (12)
Sandhurst School

NEW YORK

If you look out onto the City of New York,
Onto the skyline where maybe you once walked,
You'll see something missing, unseen, not there,
It may to you just seem a bit bare
The twin towers, the victims, all are now gone,
No one in the towers survived, not one.

Those helpless victims who were on those hijacked planes
Are gone forever, things won't be the same.
The feelings they can't just push aside and hide
Those heroes who search through the rubble, day and night,
Searching for life they may never find.

The hatred is great for those few men,
For all we know they may do this again.
For a three-minute silence was held with respect
For this one day those men will regret.
So if you ever look out onto the City of New York
Look at it closer, stop, think and pray,
For all the victims of the tragedy on that
                        one sorrowful day.

Hayley Parkinson (12)
Sandhurst School

RACIST ABUSE

James is sad and has bruises to show it.
They wait for him at the school gate to empty his wallet,
He bellows in his room covering the truth with lies,
His parents don't realise when he comes down with red eyes.

When James walked to school, he hoped in disbelief
Hoping the bullies had turned over a new leaf.
He started feeling sick already knowing
They were there, his walking was slowing.

The abusers at school, how can they be so cruel?
They tell him to follow one simple rule
Tell your parents, in a week you'll be dead
Your colour will be darkened with bloodstain red.

Matt Bowman (12)
Sandhurst School

THE UNKNOWN WORLD

The black holes spin wildly consuming
Everything in their paths.
The stars shine brightly each with a secret
Or mystery we may never know.

Is there life out there?
Do they look like us
Or are they shadows that drift along silently?
Is there another world like us?
We can only question and wonder.

Shooting stars, comets, glow as they
Journey across the universe.
The moon casts eerie light
On our world at night.

The sun, the boiling ball of gas,
At the centre of our solar system.
Universes, how many are out there?
What shapes are they?
Circle, square.

The blackness hides everything, worlds, stars.
We may never know what is truly out there.

Charlotte Rose (11)
Sandhurst School

SCHOOL

School is the place where children go,
Between the ages of 5 and 16,
They come to learn some English and maths
Science, RE and drama.

They go to Tutor in the morning,
And more often than not they're late.
If they get three in one term,
They're on their way to detention.

Then off they go to period one,
Be it English, maths or science.
They listen to their teacher,
Then only do half their work.

Now after a boring period two
It's time for a little break.
Children chatting with their friends.
About what they did last night.

Three and four are much the same,
As one and two in the morning.
After that it's time for lunch.
So we can stuff our faces.

Period 5, the last in the day,
Before we get our freedom.
When the bell goes we pack up our stuff,
And then we get the homework!

James Cholerton (12)
Sandhurst School

The Old Man

His face was as dry as elephants' skin,
And his hand like rough, brown sandpaper.
He had a head of snow-white hair,
And a long, thick beard to match.

His eyes were a misty green,
Like the waves of a stormy sea,
He was a large, broad man,
With a voice as loud as thunder.

He wore grey cord trousers,
With a white buttoned shirt.
And on his feet, stayed all the time,
Black boots with heavy buckles.

He lived at the top of the hill,
With his small, scruffy mut,
Who spent all day wagging his tail,
Sitting inside - looking out.

He was a mysterious character,
Not telling a soul where he was from,
Or where he was going,
Nothing - not even his name.

One golden morning in autumn,
The villagers came out of their homes,
Looked at the empty house on the hill,
As the man had secretly come and gone.

Laura Brownlie (12)
Sandhurst School

A Cat's Life

He lies beneath an oak tree,
His silky fur gleaming in the sun,
His amber eyes staring at me,
To be a cat, must be fun.

Nothing to do all day long,
Watching the clouds floating by,
Just listening to birds singing their song,
And gliding from the trees into the sky.

Along comes a mouse wandering past,
The cat jumps up, in his eye a glimmer,
The mouse squeals as the cat snatches him fast,
That must have been a satisfying dinner.

The elegant creature returns to his home,
And snuggles up into his warm bed,
His day for tomorrow remains unknown,
While today's events stay fresh in his head.

Aimée Sheppard (12)
Sandhurst School

Virgo

The sign for a Virgo is a mermaid or girl,
With long, golden, blonde hair,
So if your birthday is between the two dates,
Your destiny will soon start here.

Generally Virgo is a very shy sign,
But they can also speak their minds,
Which is why you sometimes appear too critical,
But it's really all down to the stars.

You hate rude people and show-offs,
But like shopping for bargains,
Always searching with your mates,
And in the end you'll find one.

This is a bit like love and friendship,
Your perfect match is a Gemini,
Sooner or later you'll find your soulmate,
Whether it's true love or just to be friends.

Laurel Knight (13)
Sandhurst School

HAPPY BIRTHDAY MUM!

Birthdays have always been
A source of such delight
Birthdays have made the world so wonderful
So colourful and bright.

So Mum I'm wishing you a birthday
That's filled right from the start
With all the pleasant things dearest to your heart.

With many warm wishes,
A world of love too
Because it's your birthday
Because you are you.

But it will soon be tomorrow
And your special day will end
But I will still love you
Because you're the best ever friend.

Rebecca Sandy (11)
Sandhurst School

A Fright Night

It was a dark night,
I was in a forest,
I was camping with my friends.

It was misty and cold,
I heard mosquitos buzzing around my ear,
Then I saw a shadow outside my tent.

And then it disappeared,
I thought it was the bush,
I heard a rustling in the bush,

I came out of my tent and my friend went *boo!*
Then I heard a rustling in the bush again,
And again I thought it was my friend,

But to my surprise it was a bear
Rrooaarr! it went,
Scared already.

I woke up and it was all a dream.

Antony Walter (11)
Sandhurst School

Autumn

The autumn leaves turn reddish brown
Falling, tumbling to the ground.
It's cold and misty, dull and grey
An average dreary autumn day.

Juicy ripe plums, pears bright yellow
Rosy red apples, the season is mellow
The autumn fruits ready and so sweet
Such good taste and so good to eat.

Darker evenings and shorter days
Whilst summer goes, autumn stays.
Left with weather that's becoming cold
Before freezing winter takes its hold.

Stephanie Hayes (12)
Sandhurst School

NEW YORK TRAGEDY

Who would have known
At the start of the day:
A certain plane
Was up and away?

Led by Arabs
Bin Ladan's crew,
It took thousands of lives
And the Twin Towers too.

Up in the air
Climbed the thick black smoke,
While the rest of the world
Watched with hope.

Rescue attempts
Knew no bounds,
The people who died
Were also on the ground.

On that day
Thousands of lives were lost,
No sum of money
Could repay the cost.

Laura Rosewell (12)
Sandhurst School

SHOPPING

What should I say?
Cheers Mum, or no thanks,
I'd rather have that one,
Should I ask or should I not?
Would she pay or would she rave?

Shopping is boring,
Shopping is long,
Why am I snoring?
And singing this silly old song.

Should I ask to go
Or should I move more slow?
Should I be more happy,
Or should I stay snappy.

Dragged around like an old hound,
Should I make a sound,
What should I do?
Will I wear them or will I not?

Shopping is boring
Shopping is long
Why am I snoring
And singing this silly old song?

Silly stupid shopping
It's even worse than mopping!
Should I act nice?
And be good as gold
Or should I stay grumpy and act all old?

Shopping is boring
Shopping is long
Why am I snoring?
And singing this old song.

Chris James (11)
Sandhurst School

THE SPACE MISSION

The rocket booms,
Into the dark space gloom.
They're flying through space
In search of the new human race.

Stars twinkle in the sky,
Just like a butterfly,
They're flying through space
In search of the new human race.

Comets zooming,
Looks like a flower blooming.
They're flying through space
In search of the new human race.

Spacecraft lands
Upon the planet's desert sands
They're flying through space
In search of the new human race.

This desert feels like a city
But there's no life here, Oh what a pity!
They're flying through space
Still looking for the new human race.

William Savage (11)
Sandhurst School

SHE'S LOST FOREVER

I meant to grab her,
Before she ran,
But she was too fast,
But then not fast enough,
The car didn't indicate,
She didn't know,
It was quick round the corner,
Like a fire-breathing dragon.
She was as helpless as an ant,
Then it hit her helpless body,
And I felt a hit in my heart,
I don't understand why the car sped off?
For a minute I thought she was okay,
Then I realised, she's lost forever.

Rebecca Driver (11)
Sandhurst School

THE NIGHT SKY

I looked up to the stars above my head,
They looked like diamonds it has to be said.
The moon is up there so far away,
It changes its shape day by day.
It glistens white in the starry night,
Till morning comes and it is light.
Street lamps glow across the moonlit sky,
Showing the way to busy passers-by.
The silhouette of rooftops in the dark,
It won't be long till we hear the morning lark.

Hannah Stockley (11)
Sandhurst School

SKATEBOARDING

I like to skateboard
freestyle up our street.
Skateboarding all night, turning up the heat.

I like to skateboard
quarter-pipe, half-pipe.
I'm getting so much height.

I like to skateboard
50-50 or board slide.
Along the bar I glide.

I like to skateboard
I can do so many tricks.
I can even do backflips.

As you can see I like to *skateboard*.

Oliver Lammas (11)
Sandhurst School

THE FOREST

The forest has a ferny floor,
It can neither be entered by passage or door,
The forest grows wherever it likes,
People sometimes go there purely to hike.
Others just go there to ride their bike,
The forest canopy blocks out all light,
When you enter it goes as dark as night,
The forest trees are as tall as mountains,
The leaves that are rustling sound like fountains.

Sam Alexander Bennetts (11)
Sandhurst School

TEN ZODIAC SIGNS

Luke is an Aquarian,
Honest, loyal and friendly,
He views life through original eyes.

Hiran is a Piscean,
Sensitive and kind,
He will help you and support you.

Nick is an Aries,
Confident and quick,
The dynamic Aries will risk it all for fun.

Leanne is a Taurean,
Placid and patient,
Who offers protection to all that they know.

Matthew is a Gemini,
Youthful and witty,
The Geminian will persuade you that black is white.

David is a Cancarian,
Shrewd and protective,
He will leave nothing to chance to win your love.

Natasha is a Leo,
Faithful and loving,
Leo will encourage you to reach for your dream.

Hannah is a Virgo,
Diligent and shy,
Virgoans explore in great detail

Tim is a Scorpio,
Passionate and forceful,
Scorpians will enthral you but beware, the sting!

Miss Jamieson is a Libra,
Charming and urbane,
The Libran will talk their way out of any woe.

Alexander Hurst (12)
Sandhurst School

MY BROTHER

My brother I really hate,
He gets to stay out late,

But sometimes he's nice,
He gives me great advice,

But most of the time he's mean,
I'm not too keen,

We get into fights,
But I know he's going to be right,

I know he's the oldest,
But I know I'm the best,

And he's kind,
In his own mind,

Sometimes he's out of his brain,
I guess I'm a little bit of a pain,

But most of all he's my brother,
And deep down we love each other.

Sophie Fisk (11)
Sandhurst School

THE ZOO

I went to the huge London zoo,
And saw a furry brown kangaroo.
Who was jumping up and down,
With a big eye searching frown.
I went down the long lane,
And saw an unusual crane,
Who pecked at the huge cage's side,
After having a big slide.
I tripped over a misplaced rake,
And came face to face with a snake.
It was crushing a hollow log,
Which inside was a green tree frog.
I talked to my friend Ryan,
And then I saw a lion.
It was eating some meat,
Which was three hippos' feet.
Then on the radio a man said,
We're closing so go home to bed.
So instead of going to the gorilla dome,
I went forty miles to my warm cosy home.

Jack Hicks (11)
Sandhurst School

MUMS

Mums are supposed to be caring
Their smiles are the shape of the moon,
They're sweet, neat and tidy
And hum annoying tunes.

They always do the housework
And never have a rest,
They love having cuddles,
And calling you a pest.

Mums, they do get stressy
And they do get quite cross,
Sometimes they even seem unfair
It's like they're our boss.

Although we go through all that
Our mums are kind at heart,
They protect us from all bad things
And really act their part.

Elise Crayton (11)
Sandhurst School

THE LONDON MARKET STALL CHIME

'Come here, come here to the market stall,
Buy some fruit or buy it all!
Buy a dripping, drooling plum,
Guaranteed to fill your tum!
Yummy kiwis for 50p
Tasty and boost your vitamin C!
Buy some juicy apricots,
Buy them all! Buy the lot!
Appetising apples for 20p,
Luscious fruits as you can see.
The grapes are squishy, soft and round,
Two packs for one, only a pound!
Scrummy strawberries, a clear, vivid red,
Yummy, tasty, like I just said.
Many fruits imported for sure,
Once you've had some, you'll come back for more!
Oranges, apples, pears and dates,
Come here to the market stall,
It's simply great!'

Sophie Coster (11)
Sandhurst School

THE MONSTER UNDER THE BED

There was once a monster under a bed,
With eight red eyes and a crushed up head.
One day something hit him, it was his tentacle,
When it hit him on the head it turned him into a fool.
One day a child went skipping past,
The monster shouted 'Oh good at last!'
He gave too much time for the child to run,
Little old monster was not having fun.
Once more something hit him, it was his tentacle,
When it hit him on the head he wasn't a fool!
The child came back running past,
But when monster shouted 'Oh good at last!'
The child ran his last run,
Cos monster got out his machine gun!
He aimed it at the child's head,
And *Bang! Bang! Bang!* he shot him dead.
Little old monster jumped like a flea,
And once more he had child for tea!

Daniel Nelson (11)
Sandhurst School

AN ALIEN LANDING

An alien came down from the stars
From a distant planet, not Mars
He landed on my home
Rebuilt the Millennium Dome
And now he's selling used cars.

He sells them one by one
And uses his ray gun
People buy them for sure
Then shoot out the door
So he makes a hefty sum.

Now he's been taken away
By the CIA.
They checked him out
Examined his snout
And now he's locked up
It's safe to say.

Stuart Peter Forbes (11)
Sandhurst School

DOLPHINS

As smooth as a snake, silky, shiny and grey,
Splashing and skimming across the sea,
As fast as a cheetah running for its tea.
Fishing for fish and nice things to eat,
It spots a shoal of fish swimming
Round and round with the current,
He dives through the circle chomping,
There was a shoal of fish and now they are gone.

Dolphins soaring through the air,
Bottlenose, common and river dolphins,
They are all beautiful in every way,
Dolphins bobbing up and down,
Spending only a couple of minutes underwater.

Dolphins diving deep down,
Breaking the surface with rivulets and spray,
Twisting and turning through the air,
As swift as a bird, as strong as a lion,
Dolphins playing happily,
Jumping and diving through the air,
Sometimes I wish I could join them
In their underwater world!

Daniela Swingler-Brown (11)
Sandhurst School

NEW YORK CRISIS

As we think and feel today,
Of all the lives,
The terrible loss,
Makes everyone sad, makes me cry.

>The scene of devastation,
>Tangled metal fingers stretch to the sky,
>The struggle to find survivors,
>Draws to an end.

The pain and the stress
Ruined lives.
Minds can't function,
Too hard to take in.

>One minute's silence held in honour, so short,
>Repeated round the globe stretches into days,
>For those who risked their lives,
>So many innocent victims.

Forces now join together,
As the waiting is over,
All George Bush can say now is:
'We're going to war!'

>What will we think and feel tomorrow?
>Makes everyone sad, makes me cry!

Katy Gravett (12)
Sandhurst School

THE MYSTICAL UNIVERSE

The stars go on forever and ever,
Who knows what is out there?
There may be aliens,
Somewhere,
But we may never know,

Man will search all day,
And find nothing,
Then return the next,
To do the same.

But some people truly believe
There is something out there,
And will only stop looking,
When they have found something,

Will we ever know what is out there,
I think,
Probably not,
In my lifetime,
But maybe just maybe,
In my child's.

We may never get to their planet,
And find out about the universe,
Who knows what is out there.

Adam James (11)
Sandhurst School